CRUSADERS
AGAINST
OPIUM

CRUSADERS
AGAINST
OPIUM

Protestant Missionaries
in China, 1874-1917

KATHLEEN L. LODWICK

THE UNIVERSITY PRESS OF KENTUCKY

Copyright © 1996 by The University Press of Kentucky
Paperback edition 2009

The University Press of Kentucky
Scholarly publisher for the Commonwealth,
serving Bellarmine University, Berea College, Centre
College of Kentucky, Eastern Kentucky University,
The Filson Historical Society, Georgetown College,
Kentucky Historical Society, Kentucky State University,
Morehead State University, Murray State University,
Northern Kentucky University, Transylvania University,
University of Kentucky, University of Louisville,
and Western Kentucky University.
All rights reserved.

Editorial and Sales Offices: The University Press of Kentucky
663 South Limestone Street, Lexington, Kentucky 40508-4008
www.kentuckypress.com

Cataloging-in-Publication Data is available from
the Library of Congress.

ISBN 978-0-8131-9285-7 (pbk: acid-free paper)

This book is printed on acid-free recycled paper meeting
the requirements of the American National Standard
for Permanence in Paper for Printed Library Materials.

♾ ♻

Manufactured in the United States of America.

Member of the Association of
American University Presses

This book is dedicated to the memory of
my maternal grandparents:

Edith Tremayne Worthington, 1882-1972,
who always encouraged my love of reading,

and *Edward Stephen Worthington,* 1879-1954,
who, though our years overlapped but few, never refused
my request to hear again the story his grandfather had
told him of Edward Worthington, who had served as
paymaster for George Rogers Clark at the battle of
Vincennes in the American Revolution. Grandfather's
story always ended as he carefully unrolled his photostatic
copy of the payroll he had obtained at the National
Archives and helped me read the handwriting of our
long-ago ancestor, then a very real person to both of us.

Thus I came to know and love history.

Contents

Acknowledgments

Opium suppression in China, and particularly the role of Protestant missionaries in it, is a subject that has drawn my attention from time to time over many years. I first worked on the subject as part of my dissertation at the University of Arizona but later was distracted from the subject by the periodical *The Chinese Recorder* through which the missionaries had organized their anti-opium campaigns. A National Endowment for the Humanities grant led me to work on an index to *The Chinese Recorder* for a number of years, the first of which I spent at the John King Fairbank Center for East Asian Research at Harvard University. During that year, 1978-79, the Chinese-made film, titled in English, *The Opium War* was shown in Cambridge and became the topic of lunch-time conversations as more and more people at the Fairbank Center viewed it. In one of these conversations, Professor Benjamin Schwartz remarked that one thing we still did not know was why so many Chinese had taken to opium at that moment in their history. That remark stayed with me over the years, and although I moved on to other topics, namely *Educating the Women of Hainan: The Career of Margaret Moninger in China, 1915-1942* (University Press of Kentucky, 1995) and a history of the Presbyterian mission on Hainan island on which I am still working, I never gave up my interest in the topic of opium suppression. From time to time as I studied various aspects of the missionaries' anti-opium activities, I was increasingly struck by the similarities of the arguments about drugs a century ago in China to those in the news media in the United States today.

In Cambridge for the memorial service for Professor
Fairbank in 1991, I reminded Professor Schwartz of his remark, which he recalled; he added that we did not know
then that the United States would soon also have a huge
drug problem and that no one would know why so many
Americans had taken to drugs. I still do not know *why* individuals in any society take to drug use; perhaps it is a question to which the answers are so varied and personal that
no historian will ever be able to identify them with any cer-
tainty. But it is clear that academic interest in this subject is
growing, as demonstrated by the number of papers on the
subject of China's opium problem that have been presented
at academic conferences in recent years. This work, which
focuses solely on the missionaries' role in the suppression
campaign, is my contribution to this growing field.

A number of people have provided me with assistance in
this endeavor. Jessie G. Lutz, professor of history emerita
of Rutgers University, and Murray Rubinstein, professor of
history at Baruch College of City University of New York,
read the manuscript and provided many suggestions. My
longtime friend Christine W. Kulikowski read both the
drafts of the manuscript and the page proofs with her professional editor's eyes and made many suggestions. Gene
Slaski, academic officer of Penn State's Allentown campus,
provided encouragement and financial assistance, and John
V. Cooney, campus executive officer, also provided help.
Also at Penn State's Allentown campus, Sue Snyder and
Nancy Eberle provided secretarial help and Kay Stokes and
Kathy Romig, both of the library staff, obtained numerous
items for me. Thanks, too, to Suzanne Wilson Barnett, pro-
fessor of history at the University of Puget Sound; Daniel
Bays, professor of history at the University of Kansas; David
Buck, professor of history at the University of Wisconsin—
Milwaukee; Lawrence Kessler, professor of history at the
University of North Carolina; Judith Liu, professor of so-
ciology at the University of San Diego, and Victoria Siu,

adjunct professor of history, at the University of San Francisco, for their friendship and help over the years. Thanks are also due to the staffs of the Library of Congress and the libraries of Washington University in St. Louis and Georgetown University for their assistance. Thanks to Dominik Fellner for his assistance in the final stages of the project. Thanks, too, to my longtime friends John F. and Vivian Cady of Ohio University, who have long encouraged my interest in Asia. Special thanks are also due to my mother and father, Kathryn E. and Algha C. Lodwick, for their help and encouragement over the years.

A Note on Romanization

In this work I have used the Wade-Giles romanization system, which was used in most of the source materials cited. For consistency I have used Taiwan only, instead of both Taiwan and Formosa.

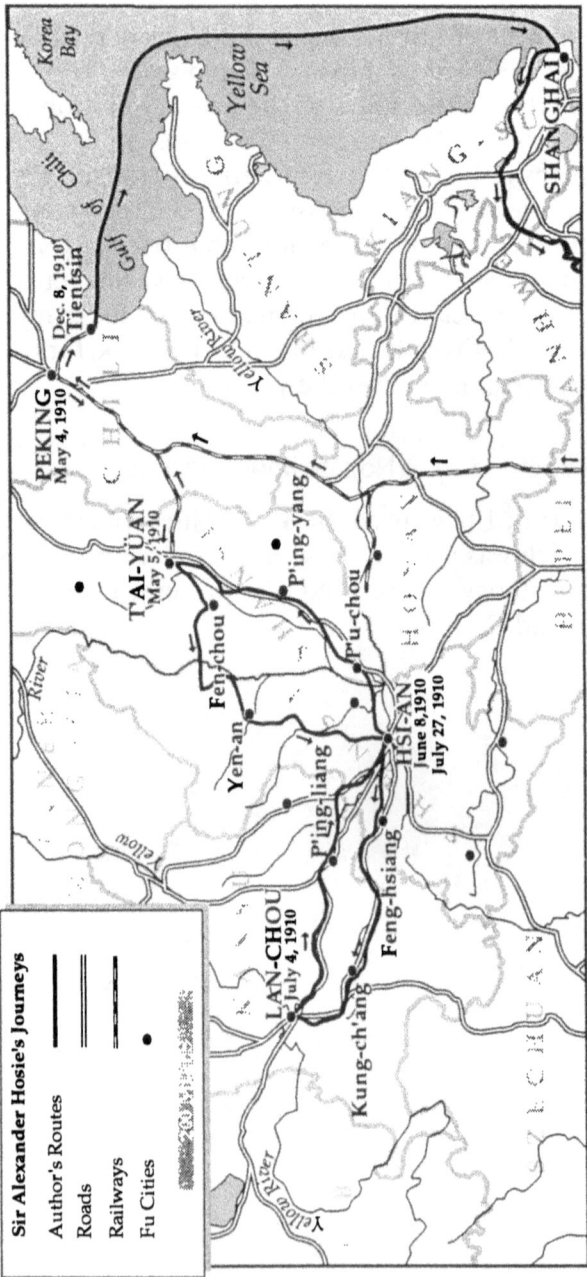

Sir Alexander Hosie's Journeys

Author's Routes
Roads
Railways
Fu Cities

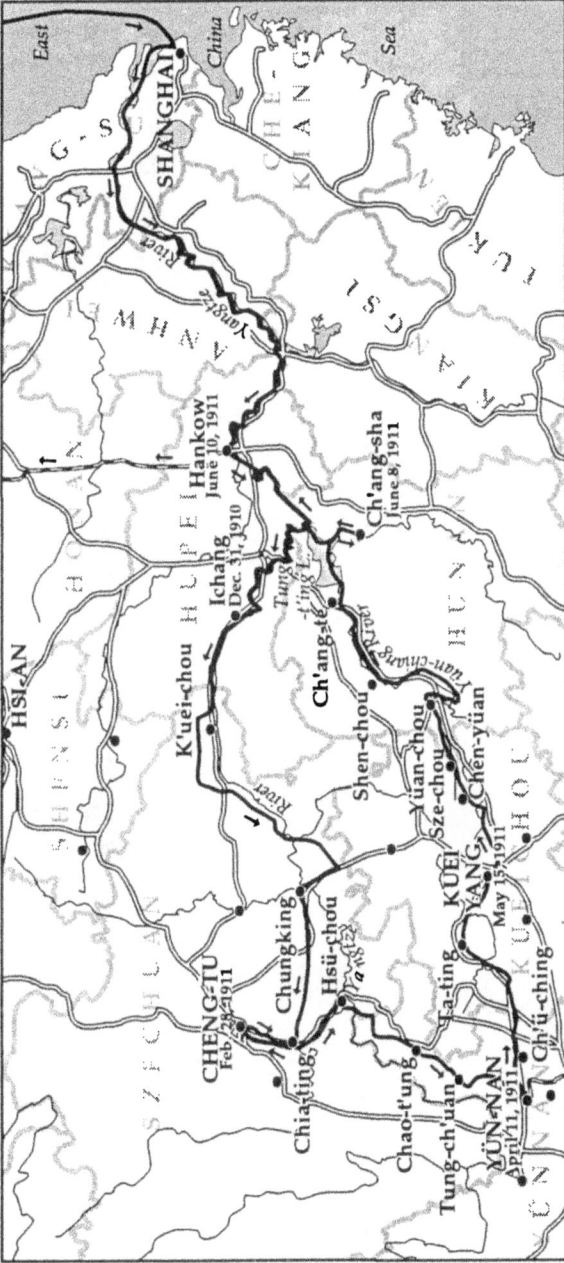

Sir Alexander Hosie's Journeys. DEASY Geographics.

Introduction

Dazzling fields of flowers, magnificent to the eye of the beholder, stretched across the Chinese countryside. Far beyond the horizon more flowers bloomed in India. Beautiful as they were these flowers were not grown to please the eye; with them bloomed international controversy, war, greed, degradation, misery, and death. These were no ordinary blossoms—they were opium poppies.

Opium was the subject of controversy in China throughout the nineteenth century and into the twentieth. No one could say how many Chinese were addicted to the drug, but addicts surely numbered in the millions, and their families, who suffered indirectly, added many more to the list of those harmed by the drug. Opium was an emotional issue for the Chinese. Its use had been prohibited by the Yung-cheng emperor in 1729, but as trade with the West increased opium imports to China gradually grew from about two hundred chests a year early in the eighteenth century to about one thousand chests a year in 1767. In 1781 the British East India Company took over the British part of the trade from private merchants, and by 1790 the company's trade in opium amounted to 4,054 chests. A Chinese imperial edict prohibited all importation in 1796, but it was openly ignored, and by 1830 the amount of opium entering China was 16,877 chests. The amount had grown to 20,619 by 1838, just before the Opium War of 1839-42. The Opium War, the first war in which the Chinese were defeated by the Europeans, was fought largely over the foreigners' right to sell opium in China. Following the hostilities, 50,000 chests of opium were thought to have been imported in 1850, and 85,000 chests entered in 1860 when the trade was legalized by treaty.[1] Once the trade was legalized opium imports were recorded by the Chinese Imperial Maritime Customs Service. These reached a peak of 102,927 piculs in the year 1879.[2] After the legalization of the trade, domestic production of opium increased dramatically, too, and, although statistics were extremely difficult to obtain, production was estimated at 376,000 piculs in 1879.[3] Legalization clearly did not diminish the demand for opium but rather caused its use to increase yearly. Within half a century the Chinese had an enormous social problem, and public outrage against the drug finally resulted in a nationwide suppression campaign.[4]

Westerners and opium were associated in the minds of the Chinese, who blamed the foreigners for bringing opium to China and addicting the Chinese to it in an effort to weaken them so that the Westerners could gain more privileges from the Chinese government. Because it was an emotion-laden issue, most Chinese did not stop to consider that smuggling opium into China in the early years of the nineteenth century could never have taken place if Chinese themselves had not been the foreigners' accomplices who transported the drug into the interior for sale to other Chinese.

The issue was also an emotional one for some Westerners, particularly the Protestant missionaries, who saw it as an evil their countrymen had perpetrated, and continued to perpetrate, on the Chinese. It was a source of deep embarrassment for many of these missionaries that they had arrived in China on ships that also carried opium, as all ships heading to China did for many years.

Most missionaries, as new arrivals in China, had had the experience of enrolling as converts in their fledgling churches opium addicts who had concealed their addiction.

Most of the missionaries took quick action to remove the addicts from their churches and to bar addicts from membership, once they discovered that addicts were unreliable, dishonest, and generally despised by other Chinese. Yet, the missionaries were also struck by the plight of the pathetic addicts. In search of moral conquests, as well as to alleviate the suffering of addicts and to gain new converts, the Protestant missionaries embarked upon a new crusade—ridding China of opium. In this quest, the missionaries were aided both by home mission boards and by their fellow countrymen, particularly some in Britain, who were indignant that their government should have an official role in the opium trade.

Britain yearly sent vast amounts of the drug from India to China and used the revenues from the trade to finance the government of India. Even the pro-opium Royal Commission on Opium appointed in 1893 concluded, "The main purpose of the production and sale of opium in British India unquestionably is to supply the Chinese and other Eastern markets."[5] To the missionaries, such government involvement was simply wrong. Protestant missionaries spent many years in their crusade against the opium trade and opium use by the Chinese, but their role was primarily that of datagatherers and publicists.

Medical missionaries in China gathered the first scientific data on the nature of the drug, helping to convince even the most hardened skeptics that opium really was harmful. The missionary doctors' scientific evidence was used by the International Opium Conferences in 1909 and 1911-12 in their deliberations. These conferences, the first ever held, were instrumental in effecting cooperation among the various nations in controlling opium and its derivatives. To the missionaries goes the credit for not allowing the opium issue to die even in the days after the Boxer Uprising in 1900, when emotions against the Chinese ran high.

The missionaries were convinced that they were right about the harm opium did, and they had the courage not to abandon their cause.

Arrayed against the missionaries were powerful government and business interests who were involved in the trade and who argued that the Chinese wished to end the import of opium from India only so that they might monopolize the trade, and thus the profits, for themselves. The businessmen who traded in opium were not interested in moral arguments; they were interested in profits, and as astute businessmen they were wise enough not to hire opium addicts to work in their firms.

In the nineteenth century, China was not the only country with an opium problem; addiction to the drug and its derivatives, particularly laudanum and morphine, was a worldwide problem, although perhaps not as serious elsewhere as in China. Opium use differed from country to country, and medical doctors were just beginning to accumulate data on the dangers of the drug, which was widely prescribed for many ailments. After the Crimean War and the American Civil War, opium derivatives were widely given as pain killers to amputee veterans, who usually became lifelong addicts.[6] In Western countries the drug was also used in patent medicines, which were indiscriminately sold prior to the twentieth century when laws were passed restricting the movement of opium domestically and internationally.[7]

Westerners drank the refined forms of the drug or injected it in the form of morphine; in India it was eaten. The Chinese alone chose to consume the drug by smoking, and apparently this difference made the Westerners view the Chinese addicts with disgust. Then, too, addiction was very visible in China, where opium was smoked in public dens. This visible use conflicted with Western standards of propriety and added to the foreigners' contempt for the Chinese. The fact that Chinese smoked the drug, and in the process developed a craving for the smoke, contributed

An opium den in Canton, 1919. The smokers seem to be scholars. Keystone Photo from the Library of Congress.

to the English language the word "yen," meaning craving. In Chinese, *yen*, often translated as "smoke," meant—literally—a craving for opium smoke.

When Chinese students went abroad in the latter part of the nineteenth century, they discovered that drug addiction existed in other countries but not in the same manner that it did in China. They also discovered just how much contempt the foreigners harbored for the Chinese because of the opium problem. When they returned to China, they saw how extensive the problem was, and many determined to work toward ridding China of the opium evil. This type of concern set the mood for the Chinese suppression campaign, which began in 1906 following the issuance of an imperial edict. For all the missionaries' efforts and concern, when the great campaign against opium began it was led by Chinese nationalists, and the Protestant missionaries, who had crusaded against the drug for so long, were largely by-standers, although some still ran opium refuges for those who sought to break the habit.

Determining when a nation is ready for social reform is not easy, but by 1906 the Chinese were ready to try to end the use of opium. In the last years of the Ch'ing dynasty many reforms were tried, but the most successful by far was opium suppression. The campaign was perhaps "the largest and most vigorous effort in world history to stamp out an established social evil."[8] The effort was not completely successful, but for it to have accomplished what it did required mass determination on the part of the Chinese people. To young Chinese, opium addiction was a sign of China's weakness. It reminded them of past wars lost and foreign business interests in their country. In truth, at the turn of the century, China probably produced eight times as much opium as it imported, but that fact was usually overlooked by the Chinese. There had been anti-opium proclamations from the Chinese government for nearly two hundred years, but what made the Chinese people willing to obey the edict of 1906?

The answer is not simple, but it lies partly in emerging Chinese nationalism and all it implied. Chinese now wanted China to be strong and able to determine its own course. Perhaps many Chinese really *saw* the opium addicts for the first time in the years following the Boxer Uprising. Those who wanted China to be a modern nation realized that achieving that ideal meant all Chinese had to be involved in creating the new state. Perhaps the victory of Japan over Russia in 1905 infused the Chinese with new determination. The Japanese had demonstrated that Asians were not inferior to Westerners. Perhaps the denunciation of Chinese society contained in the report of the United States' Philippine Commission on Opium, which was published in 1905 and which angered many Chinese, aroused them to seek to eradicate opium from their country. The report said there was no Chinese nation, only a Chinese race. (It should also be noted that the Philippine Commission recommended that children be taught in school that opium was a dangerous drug so that they might know to avoid its use.)

Many Chinese were determined that China be a nation accepted on the same basis as the other nations of the world. Perhaps, too, many officials whose responsibility it became to stop poppy cultivation and opium use finally realized what great harm it did to China. Opium addicts, weakened by their years of addiction, were seen as a hindrance to the new society. Although many Chinese had decided opium addiction had to cease, the task was not an easy one. The addicts all condemned their habits and were always ready to give up the drug—tomorrow. In the new nation being created, the addict had to be convinced to give up the drug *today*. Merchants had to be convinced to forgo the profits of the opium business, farmers had to be convinced to give up the sure profit from poppies for the uncertainties of other less lucrative crops, and the government had to find new sources of revenue to replace the taxes it collected from opium. Yet, despite these difficulties, opium eradication was one reform of the late Ch'ing years that enjoyed an immediate and high degree of success. Many other reforms of the post-Boxer period, such as the constitutional or educational ones, by their very nature could not be quickly visible. Evidence of opium reform was. That the Chinese could arouse people to take action against opium surprised many foreigners. Perhaps more than anything else, the fervor the Chinese exhibited over opium eradication convinced the foreigners that a new China was emerging and that this new nation was not going to accept foreign domination. The event that signaled the new era was the International Opium Commission meetings held in Shanghai in 1909.

For years, medical missionaries had been accumulating information to prove that the physiological effects of opium use were debilitating, and when their overwhelming evidence could no longer be ignored, the nations of the world decided to control the international trade in opium. Governments realized that opium and other dangerous drugs had to be internationally supervised if any nation were to be free from the threat of wide-scale addiction. That a new era for China had emerged was evident at the 1909 conference, where the Chinese participated on the basis of equality. One Chinese delegate commented as the conference ended that it had been the first international conference that China had participated in without having to cede territory or pay an indemnity.[9]

The story of opium suppression in China is a many-sided one involving Chinese nationalists and reformers, British social activists who took up the anti-opium crusade soon after the abolition of slavery, and various governments which were involved in the efforts to control the international movement of opium and other dangerous substances. This book focuses only on the role of the Protestant missionaries in China in the opium suppression campaign. They were the one who gathered the medical evidence to demonstrate that opium was a pernicious drug. They campaigned for decades to convince the British government to end its involvement in the opium trade from India. And it was the missionaries who saw their carefully gathered evidence of the dangers of opium used by the delegates of the first international conferences, which sought to regulate the traffic in opium and other drugs. More than any other group at the turn of the twentieth century, the Protestant missionaries in China truly understood the nature of opium addiction and had the courage to pursue their campaign against the drug until they finally convinced others of the correctness of their position.

If few were willing to acknowledge that the missionaries had been right about opium all along, at least the missionaries could pride themselves that they had finally prevailed. The Protestant missionaries alone had an altruistic interest in the issue; everyone else—poppy farmers, opium traders, government officials—had a monetary interest in continuing the trade. The addicts, of course, had a physiological dependence on the drug, which medical doctors, most of them missionaries, were only beginning to understand and try to treat.

The story of the efforts to rid China of opium in the early years of the twentieth century is relevant to the closing years of the century. The arguments of the pro-opium advocates—"we are only meeting a need," "farmers earn more money from opium than from food crops," "if we do not make money, someone else will"—have a familiar ring in the late twentieth century. Yet no one in the closing years of this century would argue, as many did in the late nineteenth century, that opium is a harmless drug or that some people need it to survive. How much has been learned about harmful drugs in the last century is evidenced by the 1899 survey of medical doctors in China, in which four reported that Chinese had told them babies could be born addicted to opium. None of the four ventured to state that they themselves could confirm such reports.

No one knows precisely why so many Chinese took to opium smoking in the nineteenth century, but they did so to such a degree that they weakened their army so that it could no longer successfully defend the country. Opium sapped the strength of the Chinese in many ways, and foreigners were willing to take advantage of those weaknesses. In China, legalization, which came in 1860, clearly resulted in more addicts each year. Many people, including all the Protestant missionaries, cried out against the use of the

drug, but a serious effort to eradicate its use in China did
not come until the Chinese themselves recognized the danger of the drug and what it was doing to their country. Intense moral outrage by a significant proportion of the population resulted in the anti-opium campaign, begun in earnest in 1906. Chinese wanted to rid their country of the
drug, and their government successfully negotiated a treaty
with the British to end the importation of India opium.
Even the British diplomat in China, Sir John N. Jordan,
who had sent a gunboat to enforce treaty rights on opium
in 1906, by 1908 simply wanted his government to get out
of the opium trade with as much grace and dignity as possible.

ONE

Opium in China in the Late Nineteenth Century

The origins of the opium poppy (Papaver somniferum) are obscure, but many botanists believe the plant is wild rather than the result of cultivation.[1] No one knows where it originated, but recent evidence suggests it might have been in Europe.[2] Whether or not the opium poppy was grown in China in ancient times is subject to dispute, but many authors cite the lack of a Chinese word for it as proof that it was not known in China before the arrival of the Westerners. The Chinese term for opium, *ya-pien*, is clearly a loan word from English. Part of the problem in tracing opium's origin lies in the fact that there are many varieties of poppies, some of which were grown in China.

Some credit the Arabs with introducing the opium poppy to China in the seventh or eighth century A.D., and others credit the Portuguese with its introduction in the 1500s. Hosea Ballou Morse, noted author of works on Chinese international relations during the Ch'ing dynasty, stated that the Dutch in Taiwan introduced the practice of smoking opium mixed with tobacco to the Chinese.[3] Yet, if the Chinese did not use opium prior to the arrival of the Portuguese, one might argue that there would not have been the ready market for the drug that the Portuguese found. One can assume that the opium poppy was known in China and that opium was used as a drug at least by the reign of the K'ang-hsi emperor (1661-1722), since the first edict against the use of the drug was issued just shortly after his death.

Throughout most of the nineteenth century, opium was

the major import of China, replaced by cotton only in 1890. The Imperial Maritime Customs Service kept statistics on the amount of opium imported and the taxes collected on it. Based on the Customs statistics, Morse reported that the amount of opium imported to China was 50,087 piculs in 1863; 60,948 in 1867; and 82,927 in 1879 when the trade reached its height. In addition, Morse estimated that in each of these years another 20,000 piculs were smuggled into China. The imports fell slightly, to 82,612 piculs in 1888 and then to 49,309 piculs in 1897. By 1905 imports stood at 51,920 piculs. In each of these years, Morse estimated 5,000 piculs of opium went unreported. In 1911 he reported 27,758 piculs imported with 3,000 piculs unreported. The price of the foreign opium varied greatly, depending upon its quality and place of origin and the port in China where it was sold. It was not uncommon for high quality Patna opium to sell for 1,000 Haikwan Taels (Hk. Tls.) or more in Shanghai in the 1880s. The opium arriving in China was about equally divided between the Bengal and the Malwa products that together totaled about 95 percent of the trade. A duty of 30 Hk. Tls. per picul had been established in 1858, and the Chefoo Convention of 1876 set the likin on opium at 80 Hk. Tls. per picul, making the total duty 110 Hk. Tls. The annual value of the opium imports was between 30 and 40 million Hk. Tls.[4] Sir Robert Hart, inspector general of Customs, was concerned that the free port of Hong Kong was the smugglers' chief point of entry and once suggested stationing a Customs commissioner in India to collect both the Chinese customs duty and the likin.[5]

Cultivation of the opium poppy in China probably began in the late eighteenth or early nineteenth centuries and gradually spread to all parts of the empire. By the late 1880s it was a major crop in some parts of China and took valuable land away from food crops. Because of the money that could be made from the sale of opium, many farmers planted opium poppies on their best land, with the result that food crops were frequently in short supply.

Although in India only the white poppy was grown, the Chinese grew all varieties of the plant, and when it flowered the fields were ablaze with white, yellow, red, pink, and purple blossoms. The plant is an annual, and after flowering it produces a seedpod about the size of an egg that, by a highly complex chemical process, produces opium for about a ten-day period. The pod is scratched at sunset and oozes a white, milky substance which quickly turns into a brownish-yellow, sticky mass.[6] After collection, the raw opium turns black. In India it was stirred for hours to dry it so that it could be formed into balls. In China the raw opium was boiled to reduce it by 50 per cent to make it purer.

Accurate statistics on the extent of opium cultivation in China in the late nineteenth century are virtually nonexistent, because poppy cultivation was illegal and the Chinese government had no agency for maintaining statistics on the production, which was not subject to taxation. Much of the opium that was transported from province to province was smuggled to avoid customs officials. Import statistics kept by the Imperial Maritime Customs Service show a decline in the importation of opium in the closing years of the century, and this is often attributed to the rising domestic cultivation, since the number of addicts was increasing at that time.

In an attempt to gather information on the extent of native cultivation, Sir Robert Hart issued circulars in 1864, 1879, and 1887 to the various Customs stations in China inquiring if native opium were known there, where it came from, how much was cultivated in each place, what the taxes on it were, and what varieties were being sold.

The 1864 responses indicated that native opium was known in all the ports, but few acknowledged it being grown in their areas. A. MacPherson, the acting commissioner of Customs in Hankow, reported that native opium was 30 percent cheaper than imported opium but that the difference was compensated for by the fact that the imported varieties were of a greater strength. He also wrote that hostilities, related to the Nien Rebellion, had interrupted the supplies of opium in the city.[7] James Brown at Ningpo reported that juice from the red poppy had been produced locally but smokers described it "as having an insipid taste, and as losing much weight during the boiling process of its preparation for the pipe."[8]

In 1879 C. Lenox Simpson in Chefoo reported, "Much difficulty has been experienced in eliciting answers to the various questions put to the Native Opium shops and others, all viewing with suspicion any inquiries made, evidently fearing that some prohibition is about to be put on trade, or that their interests are in some way to suffer." H.E. Hobson in Amoy reported that when one asked about native opium the reply was that it was not grown, as it was "prohibited."[9] Ernest T. Holwill in Kiukiang reported that estimates of native cultivation in his area ranged from none to his own guess of 77,000 piculs. He also reported that the American missionary, John Thorne, had recently returned from a tour of Anhwei where he noted that in many districts on the north bank of the Yangtze there were "acres and acres of ground devoted to nothing but the cultivation of the poppy. . . . Notwithstanding a heavy tax and the extortion of the officials, the people find this much more lucrative than ordinary grains." Holwill concluded, "If this be true, its cultivation is not likely to decrease."[10]

In 1887, of the nineteen stations reporting to Hart all acknowledged the presence of native opium in the trade of the ports. Only those stations on Taiwan reported no significant amounts of native opium in their districts. Tamsui officials, for instance, reported only sketchy information from local officials, who reported no native trade at the port, although some smuggling was suspected. The reported local attempts at cultivation had produced only very little, extremely inferior opium. Takow reported no local opium production but some importation by junks from the mainland that arrived at nontreaty ports.[11]

The ports on the mainland all reported trade in native opium and local production. There was a considerable amount of interprovince trade in the drug. For example, Newchwang officials reported that native opium was extensively cultivated throughout Manchuria, Tientsin officials reported production in Chihli, and Chefoo and Ichang both reported local production. Hankow reported importation from ten of the eighteen provinces, the largest amount arriving from Szechwan, which, with Yunnan, was the usual place of origin of most of the opium traded within China. Officials at Ningpo reported that local production had been evident in their area for more than thirty years, while those at Foochow could only provide sketchy information and thought native opium was not traded at their port.[12]

At Kiungchow, Hainan, officials reported that opium had never been known to be cultivated on the island, and dealers reported no native opium being sold in the port city, yet the Customs official there, C.C. Clark, stated that he had found one shop in the city that was selling Yunnan opium, leading him to believe that native opium was known, even though it had never been recorded officially or taxed; he was unable to guess at its amount.[13]

Estimating the extent of native opium production was also difficult for the Customs officials. As J. A. Van Aalst reported from Amoy, when local officials were questioned about the amount of opium produced in southern Fukien, they were told, "The cultivation of poppy is forbidden, thus no Opium is gathered." Van Aalst guessed that perhaps 600 piculs a year were produced in the region, basing his estimate on the amount of land under poppy cultivation and the yield one might expect.[14]

Although most Customs stations reported Szechwan and Yunnan opium traded through their ports, no one could accurately state the amount of opium produced in either province. Hankow officials estimated the Szechwan production to be about 150,000 piculs a year, while officials in Kiukiang estimated the Szechwan production to be only 40,000 piculs a year, and those at Shanghai set the number at 10,000 piculs but admitted they had no data on which to base their estimate. Francis W. White at Canton hazarded a guess about Szechwan, which he estimated sent about 2,000 piculs of opium a year into his province, with perhaps 200 to 500 piculs entering the city of Canton. The cost of domestically grown opium varied widely, with Tamsui, Taiwan, reporting a low of 130-43 Hk. Tls. per catty and Newchwang, Manchuria, reporting a high of 737 Hk. Tls. per picul. The average price at the other Customs ports was about 300 Hk. Tls. per picul.[15]

The amount of taxes collected on the sale of native opium represented only a very small portion of what the government might have collected, since all officials replying to Hart's circular indicated that the amount of native opium passing through their ports was only a tiny portion of the amount that was sold illegally. Many stated that opium consumption was on the rise in their districts, yet the amount of foreign opium passing through the Customs houses declined yearly.[16]

Native opium was taking over the market, but little of it was being taxed at the Customs houses. Methods of taxation varied greatly, but the duty most likely to be collected was the likin. How many taxes the opium was subject to depended upon the port and whether or not the officials there recognized the existence of the trade in native opium. Wuhu reported that previously native opium had been taxed at half the rate of foreign opium, but recently no taxes had been collected, since all native opium was being smuggled into the district. Amoy reported no taxes collected, since native opium was prohibited and was subject to confiscation. Swatow also reported no taxes collected.[17]

At the other extreme, Chinkiang reported that locally grown Kiangsu opium was subject to the following taxes: 0.64 Hk. Tls. at the point of production as a charity tax and 0.32 Hk. Tls. as a registration fee. In addition, en route to the point of sale a picul of opium was subject to 8.5 Hk. Tls. of duty and 2.24 Hk. Tls. for the grain tribute tax. It was also subject to a likin of 43 Hk. Tls. at the port. Newchwang taxed native opium most heavily with duties of 31.64 Hk. Tls. being collected at the place of production and 54.2 Hk. Tls. at the port. In addition, dealers and divan keepers in the city of Fengtien had to purchase licenses for 24 Hk. Tls.[18]

OPIUM ADDICTS

How many opium addicts China had was always a subject of controversy, and estimates varied widely. As the opposition to the opium trade grew, the anti-opium forces both in China and overseas sometimes inflated the number of addicts to illustrate more graphically the damage opium was doing to the Chinese people.

In 1879 Sir Robert Hart made a careful analysis of the amount of imported opium, size of chests, loss in the weight of the opium during preparation, and the amount the average addict smoked in each pipe (estimated at three mace), and concluded that the number of addicts totaled one million, or one-third of 1 percent of the population. By including the Customs estimates for native opium production, Hart doubled his figures and set the number of addicts at two million, or two-thirds of 1 percent of the population.[19]

It should be noted that a number of the Customs officials reporting to Hart guessed that the number of pipes one mace of opium would fill depended upon whether the addict was a heavy or light smoker. Some thought addicts smoked one mace per pipe, while others thought a mace would fill ten to twenty pipes, and that a heavy addict might smoke six to eight mace a day. The range of such guesses clearly indicates that Hart's figures of one-third or two-thirds of 1 percent of the population addicted might be off by a huge margin.[20]

Hart included in his report details of fifty opium addicts who had tried to break the habit at Dr. John G. Kerr's hospital in Canton. The addicts ranged in age from twenty to fifty-nine and had been addicted to the drug for periods ranging from one to twenty years. Two of the addicts used only seven-tenths of a mace of opium per day, but others reported using as much as six to eight mace daily. There seemed to be no correlation between the number of years one had been addicted and the amount of the drug used, for the two who had been addicted for twenty years used three and seven mace per day, and three who had been addicted for ten years reported using only one mace per day. Those reporting they used seven-tenths of a mace per day had been addicted for six and ten years.[21] The dangers of such statistics were well known, because opium addicts were known to be untruthful or imprecise about their addiction.

In the replies to the questionnaires Hart sent out in 1887, some officials offered no estimates of the number of addicts, but Tientsin reported 170 opium shops in the city and Hankow reported that at least 70 percent of the men and many women and children smoked.[22] Many foreigners besides Hart tried to estimate the number of addicts, but all were only guessing. One put the total at 40 percent of the town population and 20 percent of the country population,[23] while another cited 1,130 opium dens in the city of Wenchow in 1891, which then had a population of 80,000.[24]

There were probably more addicts in the provinces where great quantities of the drug were produced, and many foreigners stated that 80 percent of the population of Szechwan were opium users.[25] In terms of numbers, the estimates of

The equipment of an opium smoker. The ornate nature of the pipe and the lamp, the artistic shape of the palette, and the inscription on the handle of the scraper suggest that the owner of these items was a person of some wealth. Benjamin Broomhall, *Evangelisation of the World*, 1886.

addicts ranged from Hart's extremely low 1 million to the Rev. J. Dyer Ball's 40 million, the latter being approximately one-tenth of the population of China.[26] Jonathan Spence has done a careful analysis of the various numbers given for addicts and opium production and concludes, "Undeniably, opium was being smoked in China on a gigantic scale."[27]

Exactly why so many Chinese became addicted to opium in the nineteenth century is one of the unanswered questions about the society. Many people were first advised to use the drug to cure some physical ailment and quickly found themselves addicted,[28] but why people engaged in the recreational use of the drug is more difficult to determine.

Perhaps they were like the husband of Mrs. Ning in Ida
Pruitt's *Daughter of Han,* who, when asked why he smoked
opium, replied, "Oh, . . . don't you know. All the Immortal
maidens of the ninth heaven come trooping to me."[29]

Certainly China was in a time of rapid, sometimes cata-
strophic, change, and some people who had found the hal-
lucinatory experience of smoking opium an escape from
physical pain might have decided to use it to ease psycho-
logical pain as well. But such reasons alone cannot account
for the millions who became addicted to the drug. Accurate information was very difficult to obtain, because de-
grees of addiction varied and new users of the drug were
constantly falling into its grip.

For Chinese suffering from chronic illnesses, such as
malaria, dysentery, or tuberculosis, both the specialist in traditional Chinese medicine and the Western-trained medical doctor were likely to prescribe a small amount of opium,
as it was considered to be the best treatment. It must be
noted that the same prescription, in the form of laudanum,
was commonly given to patients with chronic diseases in
Western countries in the nineteenth century. The pernicious
effects of opium smoking soon meant that the chronically
ill patient had not only the original disease, still uncured,
but also an opium habit, which grew until it consumed more
and more of the time, money, and resources of the person.

It was frequently said by the Chinese that the cure for
chronic diseases was worse than the diseases themselves. For
example, opium was frequently prescribed instead of quinine for the treatment of malaria, with the result that in
areas where malaria was quite prevalent the rate of opium
addiction was high. As early as the beginning of the 1890s,
some medical men recognized that the use of opium for
malaria treatment was quite dangerous and suggested that
if quinine could be readily available at a low price the use
of opium would be reduced. Indeed, as the evidence of the
uselessness of opium either as a prophylactic or as a cure

for malaria accumulated, many doctors stopped prescribing it for the disease.[30] Many Chinese also believed that opium was an aphrodisiac, though, in truth, long-term use had the opposite effect and decreased desire.

The ravages of opium were no respecters of class in China. Most foreigners thought that the majority of users were coolies, but addicts could be found at all levels of society, from the imperial court to the beggar in the street. All ages of people smoked. Some children, particularly boys, were addicted, having been given the drug by parents who thought it would stimulate their growth or cure illnesses. Addicts were certainly not considered good marriage prospects, but some did marry, and some matchmakers concealed the addiction. Although the average life span of the addict was not long—estimates vary from thirty to forty years—addicts in their sixties who had been using opium for thirty years were not unknown.[31]

The income, general health, and occupation of the individual prior to beginning the opium habit generally determined the manner of life once the habit became pronounced. For the government official who could rely on others to manage his affairs and who had an income large enough to support his habit, addiction did not necessarily mean financial ruin. The worst problem for the officials was the time consumed in indulging in the habit. When the addiction was quite advanced, the individual might spend half his time engaged in smoking and sleeping off the effects of the drug. If the official had capable subordinates who were conscientious in performing their tasks, it was possible for the functions of the government to continue. Unfortunately, this was seldom the case. The official who was addicted to opium usually had subordinates who were also addicts. To further complicate matters, many of the yamen runners, scribes, and messengers were also likely to be addicts.

During an antiforeign riot in Chungking in 1886, a missionary reportedly asked an assistant of the local magistrate to send out men to search for missing members of the missionary's party. The official replied, "'Whom can I depend on? We have two hundred men here in this establishment and they are two hundred opium smokers, and none of them is to be trusted.' The magistrate himself was an opium smoker."[32] There were also reports of officials who postponed their duties to indulge their habits and of soldiers who took the drug to avoid dangerous military activities.[33]

A member of the gentry, if he were in good health and had substantial financial assets, might also support the opium habit for years without bringing financial ruin to his family, yet many did have their fortunes ruined by addiction to the drug. Wealthy gentry sometimes had a special room in the house devoted to enjoying the drug, thus freeing the smoker from the necessity of patronizing the local opium den and associating there with lower-class addicts. Like the official, the gentry member might partake of opium without having his affairs suffer, provided he had responsible subordinates. Yet, as with the official, such cases were rare; the addicted gentry member frequently had subordinates and other family members who were also addicts. If the responsible, adult members of the family all became addicted to the drug, their assets soon dwindled away as a result of mismanagement or duplicity on the part of servants.

Women addicts were apparently most numerous among the gentry class, probably because they had the money and the leisure to indulge in the drug. It was generally believed that gentry women became addicts following the examples of their husbands. In Szechwan, one missionary reported it was considered polite for gentry women to offer women guests opium to smoke.[34]

Peasant addicts and their families were the most pathetic. If the life of the peasant woman portrayed in Ida Pruitt's

Daughter of Han was typical of addicts and their families their lives were indeed difficult. Frequently, peasants' financial resources were small prior to becoming addicted and were quickly eroded by the opium habit. For example, if the peasant's cash income was sufficient to purchase the daily requirement of opium when beginning use, it was soon inadequate, as more and more money was needed to purchase the drug as the addiction developed. If a man did not have the cash to make his daily opium purchases he began slowly selling off his assets to finance the habit.

First to go were whatever small luxuries the family had—perhaps the wife's ring or an extra piece of furniture. When the money thus gained was exhausted, the addict, desperate for the drug, would begin selling the necessities of life—the land, the house, or sometimes pieces of it—the roof timbers or the bricks. When material assets had been exhausted to the extent that even the cooking pot had been sold, the desperate man would begin selling his children—daughters first, and then the sons, starting with the youngest. With the need for opium increasing relentlessly, the addict, having no children left, would then sell his wife. Sometimes the children and wife were sold into slavery, but if they were sold to a person who was not an opium addict it was possible that their lives improved with the sale. At least they were free from life with a person hopelessly addicted to opium.

The addict, having exhausted all his resources, continued to live from one pipe to the next, earning money from whatever work he could find and resorting to begging or thievery if he were unable to find employment. Peasant women who became addicted to the drug often suffered a worse fate. If both husband and wife were addicts, the wife was usually abandoned, since she could not be sold unless her addiction could be concealed. Left on her own, the woman was forced to resort to begging or prostitution to get money for her habit. Such a course of events was most frequent among the peasants, but it was not unknown to find a large estate owner who had followed the same downward road after having become an opium addict.

Addicts who became beggars were never sure if they would have money for the opium they needed. They were frequently seen at mission hospitals and churches asking for money. Many of the missionaries quickly learned that any coin given to a beggar was likely to be used to support the habit. Archdeacon Arthur E. Moule wrote, "I have been told that some of the lowest of the opium dens depend almost entirely upon the custom of beggars. This is, I fancy, a reversal of the true story. Beggars do not support opium shops—but opium-smoking brings many a man to beggary."[35]

The physical effects of addiction were horrible. Again, the wealth of the addict at the time he acquired the habit influenced how quickly the drug produced its deleterious effects. The presence of the drug in the bloodstream upset the body's ability to digest food. If the addict were of the upper classes and had sufficient money to purchase both food and the drug, he likely continued to eat properly, at least in the early stages of addiction. Also, an upper-class person likely had enough money to purchase the drug without having to work, so the addiction did not interfere with his earning his livelihood. However, the luxury of the addict's surroundings and the wealth he possessed could not prevent the drug from ravaging his body.

For the peasant, addiction was likely to devastate the body quite rapidly because of the lack of proper food. The smoker usually was able to continue to do his normal work for a period of time after becoming addicted, but how long the person could remain functional depended upon his general physical condition prior to becoming addicted, the amount of opium smoked, and whether or not adequate food was eaten as the addiction increased. For anyone who depended upon a day's work to earn money to buy that day's food, addiction was the most devastating. Undernourished at the time of introduction to the drug, these people were quick to suffer the most pernicious effects of it.

Eventually, rich and poor addicts suffered the same fate. Physiologically, opium diminished the bodily functions. The nervous system became impaired, and vital internal organs ceased to secrete their fluids. The first symptom of chronic opium addiction was the inability of the body to absorb food. Because of this, the person who ate little and smoked much was likely to become an addict quicker than one who had plenty of food. The problems of digestion meant that many addicts simply starved. Many foreign doctors in China noted that opium addicts had few children and tended to blame this on the fact that they were interested in little but smoking. Only in the late nineteenth century did some doctors realize that opium addiction diminished sexual desires and that longtime addicts had lost the ability to procreate. Even the importance of continuing the family line was of no interest to the addict. If two generations of a family were addicted, it was generally assumed that they would be the last of their line.

Many of the foreigners in China in the nineteenth century viewed opium as China's vice but saw it as no more harmful than the vices found in other countries. Those who sought to downplay the extent of the harm opium was doing to the Chinese people frequently compared the use of opium in China to the use of alcohol in Western countries. These foreigners tended to point out that neither drunkenness nor alcoholism was a problem in China. Lacking medical knowledge, many observers attributed this to the fact that the Chinese were physiologically different from Westerners and thus were able to avoid the Westerner's addiction to alcohol while requiring opium to survive.

Indeed, many foreigners thought that if the opium trade were to end, the Chinese population would suffer even greater devastation because of their peculiar reliance on the drug for sustaining life. It must be pointed out that Westerners were not alone in thinking that there were physiological differences between the races, nor can one attribute the idea to the late nineteenth century Social Darwinists. At the time of the Opium War, Commissioner Lin Tse-hsu thought that the unique physiological characteristics of the Westerners made tea and rhubarb necessities of life for them, and by cutting off the trade in these items he thought the foreigners would agree to his demands.[36] Of course, some people insisted that opium was not harmful to the Chinese. This belief developed partly because many people did smoke opium in small quantities for years before the pernicious effects of the drug manifested themselves. All had to agree, however, that these people were in a minority.[37]

Such was the situation with opium in China in the late nineteenth century. Before many years passed, that situation would be drastically altered by social, political, and medical forces in China and in the West.

— TWO —
Missionaries Organize to Oppose Opium

As the nineteenth century entered its closing decade, the moral issue came to dominate the arguments of those Chinese and foreigners who were opposed to the continuation of the opium trade. Missionaries were in the forefront of those who wanted to stop the opium traffic on the grounds that it was harmful to the Chinese people and, hence, that the British government was wrong in profiting from it. Those in Britain who were opposed to the trade were fond of citing Commissioner Lin Tse-hsu's memorial of 1839 to Queen Victoria, in which he described the benevolence of the Chinese emperor, who sought to bring peace, justice, and harmony to his people, and then inquired why she did not wish the same for the Chinese. Lin pointed out that the Chinese knew opium was harmful and had issued an edict prohibiting its use a century earlier. He asked, "Where is your conscience? I have heard that the smoking of opium is very strictly forbidden by your country; this is because the harm caused by opium is clearly understood. Since it is not permitted to do harm to your own country, then even less should you let it be passed on to the harm of other countries—how much less to China." He pointed out that there was a death penalty in China for anyone who dealt in the drug. If foreigners smuggled harmful drugs into England, would they not be subject to English law if caught? he asked. He urged that the queen show her benevolence and stop the opium trade immediately.[1]

In 1881 Li Hung-chang brought up the moral question

in regard to the opium trade in a letter dated 24 May at
Tientsin addressed to the Rev. Frederick Storrs-Turner, secretary of the Society for the Suppression of the Opium
Trade, in Britain. Li stated he had long known of the
Society's efforts to end the opium traffic but noted that
"opium is a subject in the discussion of which England and
China can never meet on common ground. China views the
whole question from a moral standpoint; England from a
fiscal." He continued that England wanted to maintain the
source of income for India "while China contends for the
lives and prosperity of her people." He said it was the purpose of the Chinese to repress the use of opium by heavy
taxation, while "with England the manifest object is to make
opium cheaper, and thus increase and stimulate the demand
in China." He also stated that the "single aim of my Government in taxing opium will be in the future, as it has
always been in the past, to repress the traffic—never the desire to gain revenue from such a source." He continued that
the Chinese government would "gladly cut off all such revenue in order to stop the import of opium. My sovereign
has never desired his empire to thrive upon the lives or in-
firmities of his subjects."[2] Li noted that the poppy was grown
illegally in China but that the government did not condone
it any more than it condoned other crimes. He expressed
his desire that the Society continue its efforts to rid China
of the drug.

Such moral pronouncements from the Chinese must certainly have galled members of the Society for the Suppression of the Opium Trade, many of whom were clergymen,
yet these utterances tended to strengthen the argument of
many of the British clergy that the opium trade was immoral.

At a time when the concept of public opinion as a factor
in government policy was still quite new, the missionaries
used their ready-made audiences in churches to spread their
views about the opium problem in the hope that their lis-

teners in turn would pressure politicians on the issue. Because there was a constant flow of missionaries from the Western countries to China and back, there were many people who could deliver firsthand accounts to willing listeners who were eager to hear anything about China and the mission work being done there. Church publications were eager for articles that would tell their readers of the good works the missionaries were doing in China, and they were willing to publish articles about opium to which they could attribute some of the blame for the missionaries not having made more converts. The need to further the work of the anti-opium crusaders, to open and staff opium refuges, and to offer addicts the latest cures could all be used to solicit contributions for the churches' work in China. Church conferences and public meetings, as well as sessions of governing boards of church and mission agencies, provided anti-opium speakers with other ready forums to express their views, again with the hope that an informed public would influence the government to take a stand against the opium trade.

Arrayed against the missionaries were powerful pro-opium forces. Many who favored the continuance of the opium trade pointed out that the Chinese grew opium and, hence, stopping the trade would not end the use of the drug in China. To this argument one of the most prominent missionaries in China, the Rev. Griffith John, replied that it was "useless" for foreigners to argue that the Chinese would grow opium themselves if the import of the drug were stopped, as foreigners could do nothing about "the possible or probable action of the Chinese in this matter." It was the task of the foreigners "to wash our hands clean of the iniquity, and allow [the Chinese] to deal with [opium] as they please. The trade is immoral, and a foul blot on England's escutcheon. It is not for us to perpetrate murder in order to prevent the Chinese from committing suicide."[3]

The moral question was a particularly sticky one for the

British, but for many years the economic question was more important to them. The missionaries said that the trade ought to stop because it was harmful and no just government could be proud of profiting from harm brought to others. Yet, supporters of the policies of the Indian government pointed out that they could not govern India without the revenues gained from the sale of opium grown on government lands. They argued that the demand for opium existed in China and that they were simply fulfilling that demand. Further, they argued that if they did not sell opium to the Chinese someone else would, and then they would be without the revenue they needed. Indeed, many Britons saw no harm in selling opium to the Chinese because they were heathens who had not accepted Christianity and thus could not expect to be treated as Christians treated one another. In the tradition of the Social Darwinists, the Chinese were inferior people, as evidenced in part by the fact that they were addicted to opium. The arguments went in a vicious cycle.

THE MISSIONARIES IN CHINA

The missionaries played a very vocal role in the debate over the opium traffic. The Rev. Silvester Whitehead of the Wesleyan Missionary Society in Canton noted "the missionaries in China are absolutely one on this important question." He stated it was the only question on which they "equally agreed," noting they were "men of different nationalities and training; they hold various creeds; they are apt to look at questions from diverse standpoints . . . yet the whole six hundred of them with one accordant voice proclaim the opium a curse, and they tell you that the trade in the past was a monstrous wrong, and thus it is still a gigantic evil."[4]

All missionaries in China had seen firsthand the effects of opium addiction. The missionary community in China was small enough that, generally speaking, everyone knew everyone else, if not personally then by reputation. This small group was able to exercise influence far beyond its numbers. The medical missionaries were responsible for compiling the much-needed scientific data on the effects of opium addiction. All the missionaries, particularly through the anti-opium societies, were responsible for keeping the opium question before the British public and government until the trade was finally ended. But the missionaries had little to do with the suppression of the use of opium in China by the Chinese government because they were never able to exercise significant influence with the decision-makers in China. Indeed, they little understood how the Chinese government operated and never knew who had the authority to make a decision on the opium question. When opium suppression finally came to China, it was because the Chinese, not the missionaries, desired it. In addition, the missionaries had many other serious concerns—conversions; translation of the Bible, religious literature, and music into Chinese; famine relief; improvement of the status of women; anti-footbinding efforts—with which opium had to compete for their time and attention. The missionaries, especially a few vocal ones, were the publicists who constantly called the government to task for policies the missionaries considered wrong, and in this they were active for many years.[5]

The Protestant missionaries in China had two major means of communicating their opinions on the opium question to each other. One means was the ecumenical *Chinese Recorder*, published at the Presbyterian Mission Press in Shanghai beginning in 1868, and the other was the periodic regional and national missionary conferences at which representatives of all Protestant denominations met and discussed their work, their difficulties, their plans for the future, and their roles in China.

It was through the pages of the *Chinese Recorder* that the

missionaries kept in touch with one another. In one of the
first issues of the periodical the editors noted with alarm
the lack of knowledge on the part of Westerners about the
opium trade and stated that articles on it would appear in
coming issues.[6] Opium was a subject much discussed in the
Chinese Recorder in the last years of the nineteenth century.
Editorially, the periodical took a strong stand against the
use of opium, under the leadership of an American Methodist, Dr. L.N. Wheeler, editor from 1890 to 1895, and another American, Dr. G.F. Fitch, superintendent of the Presbyterian Mission Press, who served as editor from 1895 to
1907.[7]

In 1891 an editorial urged missionaries to collect photo-
graphs of opium smokers and send them to the anti-opium
societies in Britain and the United States to support the
arguments against the opium trade. "Now is the time to send
home floods of literature on the subject. Old arguments
revamped, new facts tersely put, illustrations from real life,
are all in place," Wheeler wrote.[8] A year later the editor
wrote that China was "not now strong enough to prohibit
[opium] cultivation on her own soil," but if outside pres-
sures were removed the Chinese government could inau-
gurate reforms for self-preservation.[9] An 1894 editorial
stated, "It behooves the missionaries of China to redouble
their prayers in this important matter, and beseech God to
grant them deliverance from the stigma of offering salvation with one hand while with the other they hold out
opium."[10]

The Rev. William Muirhead of the British and Foreign
Bible Society, writing to the missionaries on the opium question in 1894, stated, "It has engaged your attention more or
less during all your missionary life, having been forced upon
you by the circumstances in which you are placed, and in
regard to it there are not two opinions among us." He went
on to note that "opium, as it is currently used in China, is
an acknowledged evil, a curse, fraught with misery and mis-

chief throughout the country, and producing the most baleful effects in every department of social life. Our great desire is to get rid of it, and in this we have the fullest sympathy of all right-minded Christian men at home and abroad, natives and foreigners."[11]

Missionaries forbade opium addicts to become church members, because the addicts were known to be untrustworthy individuals who would steal or do anything to obtain money to support their habits. Because they were frequently in contact with opium addicts or their families and found opium addiction to be a hindrance to their efforts to convert the Chinese to Christianity, many of the missionaries founded opium refuges to aid the addicts in breaking their habits. Some were also attracted to the plight of the addicts because they knew that Westerners were at least partly responsible for the opium problem.[12] Because foreigners had brought opium to China and the missionaries were foreigners, many Chinese blamed the missionaries for the opium curse. Much to their dismay, many missionaries learned they were thought of in conjunction with opium when crowds heckled them about the opium problem as they attempted to preach in the countryside.[13] In England in 1902, the Rev. Arthur E. Moule, archdeacon of the Church Missionary Society, told the Society for the Suppression of the Opium Trade that frequently when preaching to the Chinese, "someone shouts out, 'Who sells Opium?' My answer has been, I fear, not a very Christian answer, 'Who smokes the Opium?' I have thus silenced them hundreds of times."[14]

An editorial in the *Chinese Recorder* in 1892 summed up the problem by quoting a missionary from Fukien who thought it was utterly hopeless to engage in missionary work "in localities where the people are almost universally addicted to the drug." Although some cases of "deliverance by Divine grace from the power of evil appetite" were known, "the unreliability of converts in general who have been Opium smokers is a well-known fact." The editorial continued, "We recoil in horror from that term now coming into use in some parts of China, 'Jesus opium.' And yet these words express the almost universal Chinese idea with reference to the foreign drug. To say that this state of things does not seriously hinder the progress of missions, is to call darkness light and evil good."[15] Other missionaries found the opium question so personally embarrassing that they were reluctant to admit they were citizens of the nations that engaged in the trade.[16]

The missionaries chose various ways to oppose opium. In some cases, individuals took stands against the opium trade, and many were able to convince church conferences to oppose it. Dr. John Fryer of the London Missionary Society, one of the education editors of the *Chinese Recorder*, organized in 1895 an essay contest to expose the evils of Chinese society—"opium, footbinding, and the literary examinations"—in the manner that the novel *Uncle Tom's Cabin* had exposed the evils of slavery in the United States.[17] Seven prizes ranging from eight to fifty dollars (U.S.), were to be awarded. One hundred fifty manuscripts were received, many from students in Christian schools. They ranged in length from several pages to a six-volume work by a professional novelist.[18] Eventually, thirteen prizes totaling two hundred dollars (U.S.) were awarded, but the editors noted that little new information was contained in any of the essays.[19]

The missionaries' other means of communication were their interdenominational conferences. The most important of these were the national conferences, such as the one held in 1890 in Shanghai. At this meeting the problem of opium was dealt with at one of the sessions, with letters from the Society of Friends (Quakers) of Great Britain being read. Authors of the letters deplored the opium trade and indicated that interest in stopping the trade had been increasing in Britain for several years. Quakers had long been active in opposing the trade and in 1874 under the leadership of Edward Pease had founded the Anglo-Orien-

tal Society for the Suppression of the Opium Trade.[20] A letter from a committee of the Society urged the missionaries
to include in the reports they sent to the mission boards at
home information on the opium habit and the role the British government played in the trade. The missionaries were
urged to promote anti-opium societies in China and to send
news of their activities to the societies in Britain. They were
also asked to pray that the rulers of Britain and India would
end the national sin of the opium trade. They were also to
pray that the Christian public in Britain would be enlight-
ened as to the nature of the trade, that Chinese authorities
would take action to end the domestic growth of poppies,
and that China would end opium importation despite the
large revenue gained from it. The missionaries were also
requested to appoint a committee of the conference to send
news of opium to the societies at home.

Other aspects of the meeting included the reading of
papers on the problems of running opium refuges and the
extent of the opium evil in China. The dangers of the use
of morphine as an opium cure were discussed by Dr. W.H.
Boone. The China Medical Missionary Association asked
the conference to seek ways to stop the dispensing of morphine and anti-opium pills, many containing morphine, by
both missionaries and Chinese Christians. Dr. Alexander
Lyall of the English Presbyterian Mission in Swatow reported that the anti-opium pills, known as "Jesus opium,"
had already spread from Hong Kong into his area of Kwangtung province.[21]

The missionaries attending the 1890 Shanghai missionary conference also discussed the problems they faced since
many Chinese still associated Christianity and opium, in
part because of the unfortunate circumstance that early
Protestant missionaries had arrived in China on opium clip-
pers. They noted increasing difficulty in communicating
their views to Chinese officials. Previously, they had been
able to memorialize Li Hung-chang on the opium problem

through the American minister, but the 1881 treaty between the United States and China, which prohibited Americans from engaging in the opium trade, had closed this avenue since the American minister no longer wanted to appear as interfering in the commercial interests of Great Britain. The missionaries noted with alarm that when they had arrived in China nearly half a century earlier there were only two million adult men who smoked opium, but at the time of the conference there were twenty million men, women, and children using the drug.[22]

After much discussion and many compromises, the conference voted a resolution, the wording of which was "studiously temperate," continuing their opposition to the opium traffic, urging Christians in China to arouse public opinion against it and Christians around the world to pray for the end of the opium trade, as well as the morphia trade, which was increasing. They also agreed to establish the Permanent Committee for the Promotion of Anti-Opium Societies. The members of the committee were John G. Kerr, M.D., American Presbyterian Mission in Canton; B.C. Atterbury, M.D., American Presbyterian Mission in Peking; Archdeacon Arthur E. Moule, Church Missionary Society in Shanghai; Henry Whitney, M.D., American Board of Commissioners for Foreign Missions in Foochow; the Rev. Samuel Clarke, China Inland Mission in Kweiyang; the Rev. Arthur Shorrock, English Baptist Mission in Taiyuan; and the Rev. Griffith John, London Mission Society in Hankow.[23]

One of the interesting aspects of the all-China mission conferences was that their work did not end when the conferences adjourned. The desire of the missionaries that their ideas be carried out caused them to form "continuation committees" that were assigned tasks to assure that action would be taken on whatever matters had been approved by the conferences.

Regional missionary conferences were also forums for opposition to the opium trade. At a Canton conference in

1891 a committee on the opium traffic reported that it was thankful for the increasing awareness on the part of Christians in Britain, where the issue had been discussed recently in Parliament. The conference noted with alarm the increasing use of opium in China and elsewhere in Asia and the fact that many of the British colonial governments, particularly those in India, Hong Kong, Singapore, and Penang obtained a considerable portion of their revenues from the opium trade. The complete prohibition of opium in Japan and Korea was cited as evidence that the drug could be controlled. The committee noted that "the Christian Church in China is practically an anti-opium society" and urged that members work to save victims of the habit and to prevent others from becoming addicts. Conference attendees were urged to work for the suppression of both the opium trade and the cultivation of the poppy in China. Christians were asked to communicate with the Chinese and foreign, secular and religious press to disseminate knowledge on the opium question and to petition the British and the Chinese governments to stop the opium traffic and opium use.[24] The *Chinese Recorder* reported on this conference and in an editorial in the same issue pointed out that the Chinese government tolerated the domestic growth of the poppy for the revenue it obtained but stated that the Indian drug was much "stronger and more poisonous" because the efforts of chemists had improved the Indian drug.[25]

Two years later another regional missionary conference was held in Shansi. Those attending this meeting adopted a resolution stating "that as far as we can judge opium has most seriously damaged, physically and morally, a large proportion of the population of this province; has sadly crippled legitimate trade, and threatens yet more serious consequences in the future." The conference viewed "with alarm the indiscriminate sale in opium refuges and otherwise of medicines containing opium and its alkaloids, and urge[d] every Christian in the province to do his utmost to put an end to the practice."[26] Missionaries in India also took a strong stand against the opium trade, and the Decennial Missionary Conference held in Bombay in 1893 adopted a resolution condemning the trade.[27]

When the British government appointed a royal commission in 1893 to investigate the opium question, the missionaries were elated until they learned that the Royal Commission on Opium would study the question in India but not in China. As the commission began its work, the China missionaries quickly found their opinions were going to be ignored and the anti-opium societies, which in many cases had been fostered by the Women's Christian Temperance Union, were too casually organized and lacked the funds required to send telegrams to the commission to attempt to correct the situation.

Accordingly, a plea went out in the *Chinese Recorder* for money from anyone in China and Britain who wished to have the views of the China missionaries expressed to the commission. Largely as a result of their dealings with the commission, many missionaries realized the need to develop a national organization to combat the opium problem. Thus in June 1896, the missionaries in China proposed an anti-opium league, to be "composed of representatives of all the missionary communities in the empire, along with all who sympathize with its objectives and are willing to lend a helping hand." The objectives of the league were "1. To cooperate with the Society for the Suppression of the Opium Trade [in Britain]. 2. To collect information and statistics as to the effects of opium use in China. 3. To inform the Christian people of the countries from which we come concerning the evils of opium, and to enlist their prayers, sympathy and efforts in behalf of this cause. 4. To agitate the anti-opium question among the Chinese themselves and to enlist the aid of those who sympathize with our object."[28]

The Anti-Opium League in time had a few Chinese members, but it was primarily a missionary organization, and missionaries served as its officers throughout its existence. The idea for the league grew out of the 1890 Missionary Conference and the work of an anti-opium group in Soochow, which had formed a committee in February 1896 to correspond with other missionary communities on the opium question. In December 1896, the Soochow group proposed a national meeting to be held in Shanghai the following year. All local anti-opium societies were urged to register with the Shanghai Missionary Conference so that there might be a record of the groups in existence.

The Provisional Executive Committee of the Anti-Opium League was composed of the Rev. Hampden C. DuBose, American Presbyterian Mission in Soochow; Duncan Main, M.D., Church Missionary Society in Hangchow; William H. Park, M.D., American Southern Methodist Mission in Soochow; the Rev. George L. Mason, American Baptist Missionary Union in Huchow, Chekiang; and the Rev. John N. Hayes, American Presbyterian Mission in Soochow.[29] The close relations of the entire missionary community, scattered across the whole of China, and the influence of the *Chinese Recorder* as their means of communication, were well demonstrated in the case of the Anti-Opium League, which was proposed, came into existence, adopted goals, elected an executive committee, and set a time and place for its first meeting all within the space of one year through the pages of the publication. When the league met for the first time in Shanghai on 23 September 1897, its major work was to propose that a pamphlet be issued giving the views of missionary doctors on the effects of opium use by the Chinese. All were convinced of the harm opium did to the Chinese, and the league saw anti-opium writing as its major work. The task before them was to convince the people in their home countries of the correctness of their views and to obtain support in the crusade against opium.

A pamphlet was to be compiled by William H. Park, M.D., of the Soochow Hospital. Questionnaires were sent "to all

the (Western) doctors in China so far as known."[30] (A list of
the questions asked appears in the Appendix.) In case anyone had been missed, the questions were published in the
Chinese Recorder. The results of the survey were published
in both Chinese and English in 1899 under the title *Opinions of Over 100 Physicians on the Use of Opium in China*. A
free copy was sent to every missionary in China. Most of
the 106 doctors who replied to the questionnaire were missionaries who practiced among the Chinese. Twenty-five of
the doctors were women and four were Chinese who had
been educated in Western countries. All the doctors except
two, practicing among foreigners at Shanghai, spoke Chinese. Replies from doctors on Taiwan were also included.
The years the doctors had practiced in China ranged from
one to forty-four, with the average being nine. Together they
saw some 750,000 patients in a year.[31]

Asked to describe the moral, physical, and social effects
of opium on its users, one doctor commented "bad, *utterly
bad*," while another replied, "Morally—demoralizing, Physically—weakening, Socially—degrading." Other responses
were "Ruin"; "Opium ruins the consumer morally and physically, and if money fails, his social position is ruined also.
Some rich receive no injury in any way"; "Have seen no good
effects except in cases of *incurable* pain where it afforded
relief"; and "No one can live amongst opium smokers without the unpleasant conviction that in all three points its ravages are deplorable. It destroys morals, makes physical
wrecks and severs social relationships."[32]

In reply to the question "What are the proportions of
those who smoke opium: A. Without injury? B. With slight
injury? C. With great injury (opium sots)?" most of the
doctors said few or none smoked with no injury. Those suffering slight injury were estimated between "very few" and
"the majority." The most commonly cited figures were 30
to 50 percent and the highest was 80 percent, reported by
one of the physicians whose practice was confined to the

foreign community at Shanghai. Those who suffered great injury and became opium sots were estimated to number between 5 percent and "all who continue the habit."[33] The difficulty with the statistics stemmed from the contact the doctors had with opium addicts. Many found that addicts gave unreliable answers when questioned about their addiction. Quite often the doctors were unsure how long a person had been using opium or how much was used.

All the doctors reported that opium smoking was increasing in their districts or remaining steady, and one cited the decline in price as the probable cause. Only Dr. Peter Anderson, an English Presbyterian who practiced on Taiwan, reported a decline in the number of addicts, probably due to the efforts of the Japanese, who had gained control of the island in 1895.[34] Most doctors reported that women smoked opium, but few were able to cite any specific numbers. The majority of the doctors thought there were few children who smoked opium, but many had at least seen some cases of child addicts; others said boys smoked but girls did not or that older children smoked but not younger ones.

Replies to the question "Do the effects of opium-smoking by parents show in their children?" indicated that little was known of childhood addiction. Some of the doctors knew of no effects upon the children, but others noted that children of addicts tended to be weak and diseased. Some of the doctors knew that opium smoking tended to diminish the ability to procreate, with some stating that if both husband and wife were addicts they were unlikely to have children. A few doctors thought the children of addicts were likely to become addicts themselves at an early age. Dr. Thomas Rennie, who practiced among the foreign community in Taiwan; Dr. James B. Woods of the American Southern Presbyterian Mission in Hwaian; Dr. Herbert Parry of the China Inland Mission, who had practiced in Szechwan and Shantung; and Dr. Park all reported that Chinese had told them that newborn babies of addicts craved opium, indicating that some Chinese, if not the Western doctors, recognized that children could be born with an addiction to the drug. Park stated, "The Chinese say the child of an opium-smoking mother cries incessantly and cannot live unless opium fumes are, at short intervals, blown into its face, and if it grows up it is almost sure to become an 'opium devil.'" Dr. Woods' report was similar. He wrote, "The Chinese say children are born with the opium 'yin,' and die often unless their mothers or friends blow the opium smoke down their throats, quickly soothing them and enabling them to nurse, which they have before refused to do." Parry and Rennie also reported that Chinese said the babies of addicts needed opium smoke blown into their faces if they were to live.[35]

Ninety-five doctors thought there was a tendency for addicts to increase the amount of opium smoked. Only six thought it was possible to smoke opium for years without becoming addicted, and each of the six qualified his statements by saying it was possible to avoid addiction only if very little opium were smoked or by saying it was possible but extremely rare.

Questioned about the prevalence of opium use among laborers, merchants, and artisans, the doctors again cited widely varying figures, but the average was about 40 percent. Some thought chairbearers were the most heavily addicted, while others thought the habit was more prevalent among merchants and yamen officials. Many thought that addiction was more prevalent among urban dwellers than among the farm population. Many thought opium was likely to increase the efficiency of workers temporarily, but it was known to be detrimental in the long run. Most reported employers did not like to hire addicts because they were untrustworthy, inefficient, and dishonest. Park reported making a sedan chair ride to the home of a patient who had been poisoned by opium. Five of his six chairbearers were addicts and were barely able to reach the destination.

At the conclusion of his business, he found the five addicts at a nearby opium den, smoking to get enough strength to carry him home![36]

Chinese generally condemned the habit as degrading or injurious, eighty-five of the doctors replied.[37] Since the opium habit was often compared to addiction to alcohol, which was common in the Western countries, the doctors were queried about this. Seventy of the doctors questioned thought opium was worse than alcohol, while three thought alcohol was worse than opium, and twenty-nine were unable to state which was worse. Some of the doctors stated they had never heard the Chinese compare the two habits and noted that drunkenness in China was not the problem it was in the Western countries.[38]

Seventy-seven of the doctors stated that, to their knowledge, opium was not a prophylactic against fever, rheumatism, or malaria, and sixty-four stated that the Chinese in their areas did not regard opium as such. However, most of the doctors reported that Chinese physicians prescribed the drug for chronic illnesses and that the sufferer might obtain temporary relief by using the drug.[39]

Questioned about opium-related deaths, all the doctors replied that the drug was frequently used as a means of committing suicide, and others died either from prolonged use of the drug, which destroyed their bodies, or from attempted cures of the habit. With few exceptions, the doctors reported suicide was quite common in their parts of China. Park noted that in Soochow suicide by opium was so common that several native physicians and many quacks made a practice of rescuing those who had taken opium to kill themselves. There were doctors at several institutions in the city who made calls day or night to treat those who had taken the drug. One of these institutions had answered 111 calls to treat would-be suicides in the first six months of 1898. Of these, forty-two of the forty-seven men who had tried suicide were rescued and fifty-two of the sixty-four women

Line drawings from a series that appeared in many publications, most likely first in a pamphlet of the Society
for the Suppression of the Opium Trade, showing the
problems of the family of a wealthy opium user.

were saved. In the city of Soochow, Park estimated, about one thousand persons a year tried suicide and about 15 percent of them succeeded. Using his figures from that city, he estimated that there were 800,000 attempted suicides in China each year, of which 120,000 succeeded. He noted that opium was the most common means of committing suicide and that these deaths, added to the 70,000 or 80,000 opium addicts who died yearly from the ravages of opium smoking, accounted for an awesome number of lives lost.[40]

Park's estimates on the number of suicides where opium was used were probably fairly accurate. The China Inland Mission station at Chunking had reported that its doctors treated at least one would-be suicide a day in 1877 and in 1885 rescued more than five hundred persons from intentional death by the drug.[41]

Opinions concerning the desire of opium smokers to break the habit differed widely. Some doctors thought addicts would prefer to be free from the habit, but others disagreed. Many said addicts wanted to end the habit "tomorrow," or if it could be done painlessly. Most of the doctors agreed that it was rare for an addict to break the habit by himself, although it was not unknown. Most also reported the use of morphia pills openly sold as an opium cure, and some noted that hypodermic injections were also known. Of the doctors working in opium refuges, most used both the sudden and the gradual withdrawal methods, depending upon the patient being treated.[42]

The question of how many smokers began using opium to cure some ailment brought responses ranging from a few to 90 percent to all. Dr. Alexander Lyall of Swatow reported that many opium smokers said they began the habit to cure some illness, but he thought this was an excuse rather than the truth. How many of the doctors' patients had been permanently cured brought responses ranging from "I cannot speak of permanent cures" to "90 percent," a figure cited

by several doctors. Gaining Christian converts was one of
the reasons missionaries became involved with opium addicts. The questionnaire asked, "What number, after being
cured, have joined the Church?" Responses included "In
my own experience, none," "Very few," and "six in three
years." Dr. Dugald Christie of the United Free Church of
Scotland Mission in Mukden reported fifty had joined the
church in a fifteen-year period. Dr. Herbert J. Hickin, who
had practiced in Hangchow, Tachow, and Ningpo, perhaps
reflected the attitudes of many missionaries concerning
former addicts when he stated, "Very few. The danger of
relapse is so great that we do not care to admit them into
the church, and those who have been admitted have many
of them relapsed." Others reported former addicts had become faithful church members, particularly if they had
wanted to join the church and had given up the opium habit
primarily to be accepted into membership.[43]

General remarks from the missionaries indicated the extent of opium use and its effects upon the Chinese. Dr. H.
Mather Hare of Chengtu reported, "In this city of less than
100,000 people, there are seven hundred families making
their living by boiling opium for sale." Dr. Robert J.
Coltman of the American Presbyterian Mission in Chinan
stated, "I scarcely ever used any form of opium in my practice for any disease, as I fear the 'yin'." Dr. Mary Gale of
the Women's Missionary Union in Shanghai related a story
of addiction among the rich. A family she knew married
their "beautiful, healthy daughter of fifteen or sixteen years
of age . . . to a young man in a wealthy family in which the
father and six sons were all opium addicts. The groom, pale
and emaciated, with indigestion and insomnia, came for
treatment, but soon wearied of the effort at a cure of his
bad habit," she wrote. The youngest son, just six years old,
"died shortly, a withered little old man." Before long the
"pretty, healthy young bride joined the daily opium de-

bauch." Also at Dr. Gale's hospital she at one time had for
treatment "a mother and daughter, of sixteen, for the cure
of the opium habit. After a week's treatment the daughter
ran away. The mother remained until cured, but on going
home shortly relapsed. Her excuse was that she could not
resist the constant sight and odor of opium in her house."
Dr. Henry M. McCandliss, an American Presbyterian sta-
tioned on the island of Hainan, stated, "I think [opium] is
the judgment of God on a dishonest race."[44]

The doctors were also asked to estimate the poppy
cultivation in their areas, but the most accurate statistics
anyone could give were those obtained from the Customs
houses. Park believed that the Chinese grew poppies primarily to drive the foreign opium out of China so that
the Chinese could profit from the sale of the drug. He
stated that as long as the foreign opium trade continued
the Chinese would not listen to the foreigners who advocated stopping the use of opium by eliminating the poppy
fields from China. He thought the Chinese would see any
anti-opium agitation on the part of the foreigners as simply a disguised attempt to regain the opium market for
themselves.[45]

While Park was compiling the materials for his pamphlet,
the other work of the Anti-Opium League continued. The
Rev. DuBose called for anti-opium meetings to be held
throughout China in May 1898 and urged that Chinese officials and gentry who were interested in the movement be
invited to attend. He noted that Ningpo had "a very effi-
cient native organization" that opposed opium.[46] He also
noted that both Christian and non-Christian Chinese would
be interested in these meetings. The anti-opium crusade
was one issue on which the missionaries in China were willing to work with anyone regardless of their religious beliefs. With every mention of the league in the *Chinese Recorder*, contributions were requested. The November 1898

issue reported the league had funds totalling $296.30 (Mexican). The annual meeting was set for 7 December 1898 at Shanghai, and local committees were again urged to send representatives.[47] At the meeting the league's constitution officially incorporated the objectives that had been set forth when the league was proposed two years earlier.[48]

Chinese became contributors to the Anti-Opium League, if not active participants. An 1899 financial report listed assets at $982, of which $583 had been collected from Chinese. The treasurer stated, "The Chinese will give if we only ask them."[49] That same year the league started a bimonthly newspaper, *Anti-Opium News*, edited by the Rev. J.L. Hendry of the American Southern Methodist Mission in Shanghai. In early 1900, Dr. Park issued a tract, which the league published, entitled, "Shall We All Smoke Opium?" It was distributed to all the missionaries in China. At the same time, the local committees were urged to "collect funds for the cause, distribute anti-opium literature, organize societies, and do all that is possible to create a local interest in this anti-opium crusade."[50]

The Boxer Uprising, which had been taking form in north China in the late 1890s and which culminated in the siege of the legations at Peking in the summer of 1900, had a damaging effect on the anti-opium movement. Prior to June 1900, nearly every issue of the *Chinese Recorder* contained news and reports of the Anti-Opium League, but in that month the news of the league ceased. The league's newspaper now appeared only sporadically. The major leaders of the anti-opium campaign were not among those missionaries killed by the Boxers, but apparently the Boxers dimmed the fervor of the league. The league continued to exist and reemerged with the same leaders after the 1906 Imperial Edict prohibiting the use of opium in China, but in the days immediately after the Boxer Uprising the league became dormant.

THE MISSIONARIES AND THEIR SUPPORTERS AT HOME

Missionaries on leave in their home countries and missionary boards of the various churches represented in China
also served to publicize the opium problem. There were
continual departures from China by missionaries going on
leave, which usually lasted at least a year because of the travel
time required for such journeys. Any missionary who departed was urged to spread the word among the homefolk
about the evils of opium, and the missionary was supplied
with all the latest anti-opium literature to aid him.

Missionary conferences, such as the interdenominational
Centenary Conference of the Protestant Missions of the
World held in London in 1888, took up the issue of the
opium trade, the involvement of the British government in
it, the question of the Indian government's opium revenues,
and the effects of the trade on the Chinese as points of discussion. The Rev. J. Hudson Taylor, founder of the China
Inland Mission, told the Conference, "I am profoundly convinced that the opium traffic is doing more evil in China in
a week than Missions are doing good in a year."[51] At the
meeting, representatives of the missions in India also expressed their beliefs that the opium trade was harming India as well as China, and they blamed the Indian government for its policy of financing itself through opium revenues.[52]

The Rev. Taylor proposed a resolution calling for the conference, which represented "most of the Protestant Missionary Societies of the Christian world," to acknowledge "the
incalculable evils, physical, moral, and social, which continue to be wrought in China through the opium trade—a
trade which has strongly prejudiced the people of China
against all Missionary effort." The resolution also deplored
"the position occupied by Great Britain, through its Indian
administration, in the manufacture of the drug, and in the
promotion of a trade which is one huge ministry to vice."

The resolution called for the complete suppression of the opium trade and appealed "to Christians of Great Britain and Ireland to plead earnestly with God, and to give themselves no rest, until this great evil is entirely removed." Copies of the resolution were sent to the prime minister and the secretary of state for India.[53] James L. Maxwell, M.D., secretary of the Medical Missionary Association of London, made a brief speech in support of the resolution, stating that Christians in Britain had become apathetic in recent years about the opium problem. He had been a missionary in China, but he wrote, "I confess I am sometimes amazed at myself, at the want of feeling concerning the terribleness of this evil amongst the Chinese." While tens of thousands of Chinese suffered from the drug, he said, "we sit quietly in England, and do not rouse ourselves to deal with it, and to protest against this great and grievous sin." He called for those at the meeting to work for the end of the opium trade. Following his speech, the resolution of the Rev. Taylor was unanimously adopted.[54]

In addition to the interdenominational efforts to end the opium trade, many of the individual churches with missionaries in China took stands against the opium trade. The Presbyterian Church of England passed resolutions at synod meetings in 1858, 1880, 1881, 1887, 1891, and 1898 calling for the abolition of the opium trade. During that period, missionaries sought to disassociate themselves from their countrymen who were in China as merchants and sailors and from the policies of their government, which caused them difficulties with their diplomatic representatives in China.[55]

Following the Boxer Uprising, the Society of Friends meeting in London said it did not condone the massacres in China but recognized that many Chinese were demoralized and had an aversion to foreigners because of the opium trade, which the British government had fostered. The Friends wrote, "It is only too true that the opium vice has impoverished the Chinese in mind, in character, in estate, and in development."[56] Other British churches that expressed their opposition to the opium traffic included the Free Church of Scotland, the Wesleyan Conference, and the Methodist New Connexion.[57]

The 1891 Methodist Ecumenical Conference in Washington, D.C., devoted a session to a discussion of the opium traffic and extended, in a resolution to the Christians in Britain, "warmest sympathy and earnest prayers for their success in the removal of this national dishonor and the abolition of this appalling evil."[58]

Missionaries of the Roman Catholic Church in China were generally not active in the anti-opium movement, and the Vatican was slow to condemn the opium trade and the use of the drug. Finally, in 1892 the Pope issued a decree absolutely forbidding Roman Catholics to engage in the use, manufacture, or trade of opium. "The use of opium as existing in China is held by the Church to be a detestable abuse, and therefore illicit," he wrote. The medical use of opium was still permitted for Roman Catholics.[59]

A Shanghai clergyman, the Rev. Yen Yung-king, who had been educated in the United States and ordained by the American Protestant Episcopal Missionary Society, journeyed to England on a speaking tour in 1894.[60] Between February and September he visited 52 cities and addressed 112 meetings, 49 of which were concerned with the opium problem. The Rev. Yen also testified before the Royal Commission on Opium, which was meeting in London at the time of his visit. As one of the most prominent of the anti-opium crusaders and the only ordained Chinese to speak on the subject in England, he was important in the anti-opium movement. Many of the missionaries in China hoped Yen's impact on Britain would stir up new opposition to the opium trade.

The Society for the Suppression of the Opium Trade used a farewell meeting for Yen in September 1894 to express

the society's views on the opium trade. Yen's visit was acknowledged as having done a "great service" to those opposing the opium trade. Yen noted that the Christian
Church in China condemned opium because many Chinese
condemned it and Chinese Christians "not only see the evils
of the Opium traffic, but they feel that the Christian Church
could not have a standard of morality and virtue lower than
the heathen standard." Yen was an attraction to many who
had attended the meetings he addressed. "Many people
came to hear him from curiosity, yet he was sure that they
went away with an interest in the Opium question." He
noted that many of the people stayed to shake his hand,
and he expressed gratitude that "those Christian friends
should show so cordial an interest in a nation afar off, in a
people of another race, another tongue, another religion,
and that they should thus be expressing their opposition
to a system of trade carried on by their own Government."[61]

Yen noted that at the more than one hundred meetings
he had addressed, only one person had opposed a resolution against the opium traffic at the Lincoln and Manches-
ter meetings and three or four had opposed the resolution
at Cambridge, but on the grounds that it was premature
since the Royal Commission on Opium had not yet issued
its report. The Rev. Yen criticized "newspaper writers [who]
sit in their offices and say that Opium [is] a good thing,
and also . . . officials in India, with the telescope turned
round the wrong way"; if they were Chinese and "saw their
families wrecked and ruined by the use of Opium, they
would 'sing another song.'" He said that "in China neither
smokers nor non-smokers had a word of praise for the drug.
Opium smokers were called Opium devils, and were portrayed in pictures which carried the idea of disgrace."[62] Yen,
"a forcible speaker against the opium traffic [whose] whole
soul was stirred by the mischief which that pernicious drug
was doing to his countrymen," died in 1898 while assisting

Dr. Park with the publication of the Anti-Opium League's pamphlet on the survey of physicians.[63]

Among the English clergy active in the anti-opium movement was the Rev. Arthur E. Moule, archdeacon of mid-China.[64] A missionary of long service and prominence in China, he published a book in 1892 in which he denounced England for having introduced opium to China and decried the presence of so many opium shops in the international city of Shanghai. On home leave just prior to the publication of his book, Moule told English audiences that the Chinese considered opium smoking a sin and hence smokers were not admitted to church membership. He stressed that it was the Chinese who considered opium smoking a sin and that missionaries had not forced the idea upon them. Since comparisons of opium and alcohol were frequently made, Moule remarked that "the only true comparison is between the use of opium and the abuse of alcohol. . . . The opium smoker is not noisy like the drunkard, he does not kick his wife. But the difference is about this, that the one kicks his wife, the other sells her."[65]

Moule went on to say that in the future he would tell the Chinese that the members of the Society for the Suppression of the Opium Trade were Englishmen concerned with helping the Chinese end the use of opium in their country. A quarter of a century earlier Moule had written an essay on the opium trade, and some people had accused him of being unpatriotic because of his attacks on England and its role in the trade. Moule said he had opposed the opium trade since that time and would continue to do so. He noted that many people accused the missionaries of going home on leave to preach about opium, but he said he never preached on the subject and never brought up the question of the opium trade in public unless someone questioned him about it.[66]

Moule also described to the Society persecutions of Chinese Christians during the recent Boxer Uprising. "One of the conditions on which a man would be let off and his life spared was this: Smoke a pipe of Opium. No Christian ever touches Opium." The persecutors, he stated, hated "Christians because of their connections with the foreigners, but they know that Christianity has a high moral creed, and these persecutors themselves know that to touch Opium is immoral, and no Christian would do an immoral act." That was one of the articles of recantation.[67]

THE SOCIETY FOR THE SUPPRESSION OF THE OPIUM TRADE

In Britain the anti-opium movement centered around the Society for the Suppression of the Opium Trade, founded in November 1874 by Edward Pease. After Pease's death in 1880 his grandson, Sir Joseph Pease, an industrialist and Liberal M.P., was the chief financial supporter of the Society.[68] The earl of Shaftesbury served as head of the Society's 46-member General Council. The council included Thomas Hughes, Liberal M.P. and author of *Tom Brown's Schooldays,* and Donald Matheson, who for a time had worked in his family's firm, Jardine, Matheson, and Company, which dealt in opium. After resigning from the firm, Matheson had become a leader in the anti-opium movement.[69]

Leaders of the Society tended to be Quakers or members of other nonconformist churches. An exception was the Rev. Frederick Storrs-Turner, who had served the London Missionary Society in China for many years.[70] Members of other churches, including the Church of England, were involved with the Society, particularly through their missionaries in China. It should be noted that those opposed to the opium traffic were not limited to the clergy or even to the churches. John Morley, who became active in the ending the British government's opium trade, was an agnostic.[71] Nor were the anti-opium activists limited to one political party, although they tended to be stronger when the Liberals were in office.

The Society's newspaper, *Friend of China,* edited by the
Reverend Storrs-Turner, was the primary organ in Britain
for both Englishmen who opposed the opium trade and the
missionaries in China who were so vocal about the harm
the drug was doing to the Chinese. Begun as a monthly, the
Friend of China was issued sporadically in the 1880s, 1890s,
and early 1900s but usually appeared at least eight times a
year. The publication contained articles on the growth of
opium in India, the reliance of the Indian government on
the revenue from the sale of the drug, statements by officials of the British and the Chinese governments condemning the use of opium, book reviews of the latest publications on opium, and reports on the progress of the Society's
activities. The *Friend of China* was also a frequent forum for
the latest missionary tracts condemning opium.

The Society was active in the publication of tracts and
books on the subject of opium. Many were reprints of articles that had appeared in the *Friend of China,* but some
were original works by leaders of the anti-opium movement.
Among the Society's publications were Joshua Rowntree's
The Imperial Drug Trade, Benjamin Broomhall's *Truth About
Opium Smoking,* and *The Chinese Opium Smoker,* which consisted of twelve illustrations showing the decline of a man
once he had become an opium user. In January 1886 the
Society issued a "Statement of Facts and Principles Upon
Which the Action of the Society for the Suppression of the
Opium Trade is Based." The statement reassessed the position of the Society, which previously had sought to oppose
the military and diplomatic pressure to which the British
had subjected the Chinese in order to permit opium to enter the country. Now the Society decided to concentrate its
efforts on ending the production of opium in India since
the drug was no longer *forced* upon the Chinese, as had previously been the case. The Society also sought to convince
both the British and the Chinese governments of the "de-

sirability of placing restrictions upon the consumption of opium."[72]

Sir Joseph Pease, M.P., as president of the Society, brought up the subject of opium in the House of Commons on 10 April 1891.[73] Citing evidence from statesmen, physicians, and missionaries on the effects of opium, he mentioned petitions from various anti-opium groups and asked that the government "no longer continue promoting the kingdom of the devil by sanctioning this detestable traffic."[74] The motion, which declared the opium trade "morally indefensible," was supported by 160 members of Parliament and opposed by 130. Some of those supporting the motion, including Sir Edward Grey and John Morley, were later to become prominent in the ending of the opium trade in the early twentieth century. As part of the debate, Sir James Fergusson, speaking for the government, said, "If the Chinese Government thought proper to raise the duty to a prohibitive extent, and shut out the drug altogether, this country would not expend a pound in powder or shot, or lose the life of a soldier, in an attempt to force opium upon the Chinese."[75]

Even though the motion did not become a resolution of Commons because of an amendment calling for the compensation of the Indian government for any financial losses attributed to the suppression of the trade, the thirty-vote majority greatly encouraged the anti-opium societies and revived interest in the opium question in Britain at a time when the missionaries in China were also urging the issue be kept continually before the public. Part of the response to the success of Pease's motion was the increasing involvement of the British clergy in the anti-opium activities. In 1892 the Rev. H.H.T. Cleife of Somerset published a book, *England's Greatest National Sin: Being Selections and Reflections on our Asiatic Opium Policy and Traffic*, in which he listed the reasons why the trade had gained that reputation.

Among the reasons given were that Indian subjects were allowed to indulge in a vice unlawful in England, opium was sold in Burma against the wishes and religion of the people, opium was sold in China where the British prohibited any local taxation, making it impossible for the provinces to protect themselves from the drug by excessive duties, and opium hindered the work of the Christian missions.[76]

In 1894 Joseph Alexander, honorary secretary of the Society for the Suppression of the Opium Trade, journeyed to China after giving evidence before the Royal Commission on Opium in India. He wanted to obtain firsthand information on the opium problem and to convey to the missionaries in China the support of the Society. He also sought to learn from Chinese officials whether their hostile attitudes on opium had changed and if and how they would work to rid their country of the drug. In April he met with Tsai Sih-ying, Taotai of Wuchang, who served as an assistant to Chang Chih-tung on foreign affairs. Tsai was hostile to the opium traffic but thought Alexander's motive was to gain some advantage for the government of India. When he realized the Society was sincere in its desire to end the opium trade, he "became extremely sympathetic."[77] Following the interview, Alexander received a letter stating Chang shared the views of the Society that the restriction or abolition of the opium trade would benefit the Chinese. Chang indicated he could not then state what actions China might take along these lines, but that he was in favor of the Society's aims.[78]

Chang denounced opium in his work, *Learn*, published in 1898, by noting that China's imports exceeded its exports by Tls. 30,000,000, which was the amount spent on opium. He said that opium had spread throughout all the provinces and was worse than the plagues of the past, since they had lasted only a short time. Opium was far worse since it sapped the strength of the user and made him incapable of doing a day's work. He said it was up to officials to set the example for the people by refusing to tolerate opium smoking in their districts.[79]

Alexander went to Peking, where he had a meeting at the Tsungli Yamen with Chang Yin-hwan, president of the Board of Revenue and former minister to the United States. Through his interpreter, a missionary of forty years' service in China, Alexander proposed that "the opium trade and the growth of the poppy in China should be brought to an end by concurrent action in India and China, gradually reducing the area of poppy growth over a period of ten years." Chang told Alexander he had met the governor-general of India, "who appeared 'embarrassed' in speaking of the Opium trade." Alexander informed Chang that it had been said in the British Parliament that China was free to stop the import of Indian opium if it desired. Chang replied, "We did stop it once, and it caused a war." He indicated that he thought stopping the trade would be a violation of the treaty with Britain.[80]

Alexander next met with Li Hung-chang at Tientsin. Li was "as emphatic with regard to China's hostility to opium as the two other Ministers" and urged that the stoppage of the Indian trade be the objective of the Society. Li noted that opium was "in the Treaty tariff" so China was "bound to receive it." Li continued that China would not take any action to stop the domestic growth of opium until the British stopped the trade, but he assured Alexander that when the importation stopped the Chinese would no longer permit the poppy to be grown in China. Li promised to write to Alexander on the subject, but the letter apparently was not forthcoming, probably because the outbreak of hostilities in Korea would have occupied Li's time.[81]

Li had, however, written to the Society for the Suppression of the Opium Trade in 1881 expressing his views on the opium trade. Although the other two officials had not mentioned to Alexander what steps China would take to end domestic production, Li had given "the most explicit assurance that if England ceased sending poison to China, the Chinese government would certainly take measures to prevent its people from providing poison for themselves." Alexander noted that the Chinese officials did not endorse his plan for the gradual suppression of the drug in China, but they did ask for the stoppage of the Indian trade. He hoped that public opinion in Britain would support an end to the trade since both British political parties "have committed themselves publicly to the position that China has only to ask for the suppression of the trade, and it will at once be accorded." Alexander went on to say, "Our dependence will, I trust, never be placed on popular sentiment or on official declarations, but on Him who works in His own way to bring about His purposes of love towards the nations of the earth."[82]

In addition to meeting with government leaders, Alexander met with missionaries and Chinese Christians during visits to Hong Kong, Canton, Shanghai, Hankow, Tientsin, Peking, and Tungchow. He also met with missionaries from Amoy, Kiukiang, and Nanking. He consulted with the Opium Committee of the Hankow Missionary Conference on the wording of the memorial he presented to the Tsungli Yamen when he visited Peking. This committee had earlier prepared a memorial to the Royal Commission on Opium expressing the views of seventeen British missionaries who had been in China twenty-five years or more. The Rev. Griffith John headed the committee.[83]

Reporting to the Society at home on his trip, Alexander noted that while the Chinese officials to whom he had talked were in favor of stopping the importation of foreign opium, not one of them had mentioned the loss of revenue China would suffer if an end to the trade occurred. However, Alexander noted that in 1871 Sir Rutherford Alcock and in 1881 Sir Robert Hart expressed the opinions that the Chinese government would forgo its revenues if the opium trade could be brought to an end. Alexander also expressed the view that it was up to the British to take the first step in ending the trade since the Chinese had previously tried to stop it in 1839, which provoked the Opium War, and again in 1869, when they peacefully urged Alcock to end the trade.[84]

As a result of his trip, Alexander reiterated the view that the Chinese were nearly unanimous in their condemnation of the opium habit. Alexander noted, "This cannot be the result of any bias due to their religion; the Confucian classics know nothing of Opium, and the modified form of Buddhism that has been incorporated in the religious beliefs of the Chinese includes no such prohibition of stimulants as is considered binding by the Buddhists of Burma. The Chinese objection to Opium is solely derived from observation. . . . It is based on moral, not on religious sanctions."[85]

After the publication of the report of the Royal Commission on Opium, the Society found it necessary to redouble its efforts. In October 1897, the *Friend of China* published a letter that was then being sent to all missionaries arriving home on furlough urging them to continue to speak out on the evils of opium. The letter stated that the majority report of the Royal Commission had "thrown doubt upon our two main positions: That the consumption of opium is exerting a distinctly deteriorating effect upon the Chinese people, physically, socially, and morally" and "that the past history and present enormous extent of the Opium Trade with India produces . . . suspicion and dislike in the minds of the Chinese people towards foreigners and is thus a serious hindrance to their reception of the Gospel." The letter asked for the help of the missionaries since "a sentence or two spoken by a Missionary, in the course of an Address on the work in which he is engaged, will be heard by many whom it is impossible to reach by any direct effort on the part of those engaged in the Anti-Opium Agitation."[86]

The Boxer Uprising caused the Society to pause in its work, and the 1900 annual meeting held on 6 April was more subdued than usual. Yet the members noted that the cause of the Society was still just and they needed to work for the fulfillment of their aims.[87] Dr. Park wrote to the Society from Soochow on 19 July that many Chinese in that area were joyous over the success of the Boxers in Peking. He quoted Chinese as saying, "They brought opium to our country; let us drive it out at the same time we get rid of the foreigners."[88]

So close was the association of the foreigners with opium that one missionary in China attributed to opium at least part of the blame for the Boxer Uprising. He wrote, "the Chinese trace their national decay and attribute their national disasters to the use of opium; and . . . the introduction of the habit is indissolubly associated with their intercourse with foreign nations, and especially Britain. These sentiments are common to all classes."[89] Sir John Kennaway, M.P., president of the Church Missionary Society and member of the General Council of the Society for the Suppression of the Opium Trade, also listed opium as one of the causes for the Boxer outbreak, although the editors of the *Friend of China* thought he was not strong enough in his point that the British had forced opium on China at the point of a gun. The opium trade was also given as a cause of the Boxer Uprising when the negotiations of the Boxer settlement began. At the negotiations in Paris, Alexander was anxious to have opium recognized as a cause to lessen the blame that others wanted to rest solely with the missionaries.[90]

Within the British government there was little support for the ending of the opium trade, and no action was taken after 1891. Too many Englishmen simply believed that the Chinese were not sincere in desiring to end the use of opium. Too often the English simply saw the desire to end the opium trade as the wish of the Chinese to monopolize the opium business for themselves, since domestic production of opium was on the increase and was beginning to replace the more expensive Indian product. In contrast to this belief was that of the Society, which saw as sincere the efforts of the Chinese to abolish opium use within China.

General elections were held in Britain in 1900 and many supporters of the Society in both parties were reelected, including Sir Joseph Pease. After the election and the settlement of the Boxer problems in China, Joshua Rowntree, chairman of the Representative Board of the Anti-Opium Organizations, sent a note to members of Parliament outlining the board's current view on the opium question. Among the points made were that the trade had been declared "morally indefensible" by a vote in Commons in 1891 yet it still continued, that the Chinese had long recognized the harm of the trade and sought to prohibit the importation of opium, that the British government in India continued the trade despite the harm it brought to the Chinese people, and that England was injured, morally, commercially, and politically by the trade. The note was signed by the archbishop of Canterbury; several Anglican bishops; the heads of the Wesleyan Conference; the United Methodist Free Church; the Evangelical Free churches; the president of the YMCA; and many others.[91]

In April 1902 Frederick Temple, the archbishop of Canterbury, forwarded to Lord Salisbury, the prime minister, another memorial from the Anti-Opium Societies in Britain, which was signed by the leaders of the Church of England, the Church of Ireland, the Church of Scotland, the Congregational, Baptist, Presbyterian, and Methodist Churches, and the Society of Friends, which stated they were convinced "by manifold and weighty evidence" of the correctness of their view that the opium trade hurt other aspects of British commerce in China, that it fostered "profound feelings of hostility to British Subjects and Interests in the mind of the Chinese people," that opium use in China was "a vast national curse," and that "it is unworthy of a great Christian power to be commercially interested, in any degree, in the supply of Opium in China." Accordingly, they took the position that it was "the grave duty of the nation . . . to purge itself anywise of connection with a great and public wrong."[92]

Because of the religious inclinations of many of the leaders of the anti-opium movement, many of the meetings of the Society for the Suppression of the Opium Trade were religious in tone, and much time was spent in prayer and discussion of the biblical condemnations of evil.[93] The 1892 annual meeting of the Society was preceded by a prayer meeting at the Friends' Meetinghouse in Westminster. The Reverend Broomhall, secretary of the China Inland Mission, presided at the first hour, which was devoted to prayer on the subject, "The Opium Trade: A Hindrance to Missionary Effort." He "pointed out that the traffic not only creates prejudice against the Gospel amongst the Chinese, but the vice which it feeds incapacitates them from receiving its blessed message." During the second hour the subject for prayer was "The Opium Trade a National Sin."[94] The letter sent to missionaries visiting home on furlough issued by the Society in 1897 began with "'A True Witness delivereth Souls' Prov. XIV. 25" and the title page of every issue of the *Friend of China* contained the words "Righteousness exalteth a nation, but sin is a reproach to any people."[95] Because of the prevalence of clergymen in the anti-opium movement and their penchant for quoting Scripture to support their position and because the most damning evidence on the havoc opium wrought on the Chinese population came from missionaries, some laymen in Great Britain, including members of Parliament, were inclined to dismiss the anti-opium movement as so much hellfire and brimstone.

The evidence the China missionaries gave on opium addicts was accurate and the Society did its best to convey the information to the public in Britain, yet the message was not believable to the average Briton. In the late nineteenth century some medical doctors were still arguing that opium was a mild narcotic, useful in the treatment of many diseases and certainly not the pernicious drug the missionaries claimed it was. If the medical doctors were ignorant of the true nature of the drug, then the laymen, who had never seen an opium addict, could not be faulted for not believing that opium was responsible for the destruction of so many Chinese lives. Indeed, even the missionary doctors in China reported skeptically that the Chinese said babies born to addicts needed to breathe opium smoke to eat and sleep peacefully. So little was known of drug addiction that none of them recognized that the babies had become addicts prior to birth, even though most of the doctors knew that the addict's entire physiology was affected by the drug.

The confusion of the layman was further complicated by the comparison of opium addiction to alcoholism. The chronic alcoholic was familiar in Britain, and drink was denounced from many pulpits, but the missionaries, themselves abstainers, insisted that opium addiction was far worse than the most advanced stages of alcoholism. To those who had not seen China's opium addicts with their own eyes, the evils of the drug were simply unbelievable. In the end, the missionaries and clergymen in the Society and other anti-opium groups served as the publicists who kept the opium question before the British public for more than a quarter of a century, and refused to allow the government to forget that it engaged in a trade Parliament had termed "morally indefensible."

The growing medical knowledge about opium and its derivatives was largely the work of the medical missionaries in China. If the missionaries were unable to influence the Chinese government to suppress opium, it certainly was not because they did not try. The commitment and fervor of the missionaries were intense, but they alone could not stop the opium trade or opium use. Opium suppression became a reality only when public opinion in Britain and China favored it.

CHINESE OPPONENTS OF THE TRADE

Many Chinese were opposed to the use of opium, and prominent among them were the converts to Christianity. A group of Chinese Christians in Canton in 1890 addressed a letter to Christians in Britain: "Now when your government plants and sells opium to minister to the evil propensity of the Chinese, you are partakers with them, and what can you say in excuse thereof?"[96] In Manchuria in 1893, the native clergy of the Presbytery of the United Presbyterian and Irish Presbyterian Missions expressed their belief that opium smoking was a sin and therefore "cannot be tolerated in the Church. No opium-smoker can be admitted until he has given up the evil habit. Not only so, but no dealer in opium, no one who cultivates the poppy, no one who sells the drug in any shape or form, even in the most sugared of all forms, as pills for the cure of the evil habit, is to be tolerated." Any inquirers who were opium-smokers were required to seek help from a foreign doctor to free themselves of the addiction, and they could be given a special dispensation to be baptized only "if the doctor certifies that to abandon the habit threatens to forfeit life." A missionary who was present when these rules were adopted commented, "Drastic enough, all this, but they know better than we do."[97] Likewise, the Friends' Church (*Kung I Hui*), which was modeled after the English Society of Friends, had requirements for membership that stated, "Opium smoking is among the sins which would form a bar, unless entirely given up on reception as a member."[98]

There were some Chinese anti-opium societies active in the movement to end the importation of the drug to China and its use by the Chinese. Many of these societies had been organized with the help of local missionaries or Chinese Christians. Yet some, like the *Ch'uan-chieh She*, were not Christian-oriented. Some of these organizations, such as the *Tsai-li* Society in Chihli, which claimed thousands of followers, asked their members to take a pledge not to gamble or use tobacco, alcohol, or opium. Missionaries, such as John Dudgeon, M.D., of the London Missionary Society, who worked to organize such societies, sought to have the Chinese government recognize the importance of these groups to ending the vice in China. At least one of the Chinese anti-opium societies, the Peking Anti-Opium Society (*Chieh ta-yen hui*), communicated with the Society for the Suppression of the Opium Trade. A note published in the *Friend of China* in March 1891 and signed by a committee of four Chinese recounted the evils opium wrought on China and said, "Myriads on myriads perish by it." They also quoted the Bible and asked why the British continued to engage in the opium trade, which brought such harm to China.[99]

The Chinese opposition to opium often appeared in unexpected forms. Arnold Foster reported that the Hong Kong government once gave examinations for a clerkship paying only forty dollars a month. The examiner chose the subject, "The Effects of Opium Smoking," for the English essay. Although the government with which the candidates were seeking employment collected revenue from the opium trade, "*every one* of these young men spoke in terms of unmeasured disapproval of the habit and of its effects upon the smoker."[100]

THE ECONOMIC QUESTION

The question of revenue was important to all concerned with the opium trade. It was one thing to say the trade was evil and immoral and caused tremendous harm to the Chinese, but it was quite another to call for the end of a trade that brought so much revenue to the governments involved.

The government of India derived huge sums from the sale of the drug, which was grown on government lands. Indeed, the British colonial governments in other parts of Asia also gained funds from the monopolization of the opium trade.

The Chinese government gained revenues from the importation of the Indian drug, although it did not tax native opium, since it was illegal to grow opium in China. The tariffs on imported opium had been set by the treaties of 1858-60 and revised under the Chefoo Agreement of 1876, which allowed for the collection of the likin at the point of entry to China, but imports declined after 1880 as the native drug began to supplant the imported drug. Yet the amount of opium imported caused the Chinese serious concern. In Canton, imported opium sold for five to six hundred dollars per picul in 1889 and 23,000 piculs were imported, for which the Chinese paid $12 million. That sum was one-seventh the amount of the industrial production of export goods in the province. Those who were alarmed at the amount spent on opium urged that anti-opium propaganda be used as a means of curtailing the expenditure.[101] In 1890 Kiangsu, Anhwei, Kiangsi, and Hupeh together spent Tls. 5,300,000 on opium, of which the Chinese government got one-third and the rest went to India.[102]

Opium was important in ways other than taxation. At least one official of the Customs service noted that the drug was being used as a means of exchange. In 1887 an official of the Hankow Customs House reported that in both Szechwan and Yunnan, where cash and silver were scarce, opium was carried in place of money and used in barter. Travelers carried their funds in opium, as did students on their journeys to Peking, selling along the way whatever they needed to meet their expenses.[103]

Some British industrialists were worried that opium hindered their ability to sell other goods in China. In 1898 the Chamber of Commerce of Blackburn, Lancashire, sent a commercial mission to China under the leadership of F.S.A.

Bourne of Her Majesty's Consular Service in China. The purpose of the mission was to explore possible markets for British goods. Bourne reported that opium was the means by which Yunnan paid for the salt, cotton, tobacco, and foreign goods received from Szechwan and Hong Kong. He noted that the people of Yunnan preferred imported cottons from Lancashire, but their addiction to opium made it difficult for them to obtain the funds necessary to buy the cloth. The *Friend of China* editorialized that the "hope for British commerce is the reclamation of the people from the Opium vice."[104]

THE MORAL ISSUE

In the late nineteenth century both Chinese and foreigners were opposed to the opium trade and the use of opium on moral grounds. The Christians in Britain had been lectured on the immorality of the trade by Chinese, like Li Hung-chang, whom they considered heathen. In time many of the missionaries realized that one's religion had little to do with one's opposition to opium and even non-Christians could be useful in helping the campaign to stop the use of the drug in China. Although the primary purpose of the missionaries was to convert the Chinese to Christianity, their desire to rid China of opium, first brought by their own countrymen, led them to engage in activities that had little direct connection to the winning of converts. Indeed, the missionaries, as well as Chinese Christians, recognized that completely reformed opium addicts were rare, and since most were untrustworthy, few were ever accepted into the church.

The missionaries devoted much ink and energy to the task of convincing the people of Britain that the opium trade of the government was sinful and hence ought to be stopped. Partly because their denunciations of the opium trade sounded like sermons complete with Scriptures to

prove the evil nature of the trade and partly because the
missionaries and the groups that supported their cause
lacked access to the decision-making centers of the government, for many years the missionaries' message fell on deaf
ears. Yet, the missionaries served as a conscience, particularly of the British government, constantly reminding its
leaders that the opium trade was un-Christian, to say the
least.

Medical doctors in China, most of whom were missionaries, were opposed to opium to the extent that some even
refused to use any form of the drug in their practices. Medical science had not progressed to the point that addiction
was fully understood, but the doctors in China had seen
enough firsthand evidence of the drug's effects to convince
them that there was no such thing as a moderate opium
smoker or an addict who did not suffer physiological damage from the drug.

Many Chinese recognized the harm opium brought to
their country, and they opposed the use of opium in increasing numbers as the century neared its close. Anti-
opium societies, most with missionary connections, were
founded. Chinese officials, such as Chang Chih-tung and
Li Hung-chang, opposed opium use, but they were unable
to offer concrete plans for ending the use of the drug in
China. In the last years of the Ch'ing dynasty, when many
more Chinese came to realize the harm opium wrought,
the movement to suppress the drug gained momentum.

In Britain, the Society for the Suppression of the Opium
Trade was active for more than a quarter of a century in
trying to get the British government to stop the opium trade
from which the government of India obtained much revenue. Like the missionaries in China, the Society could not
stop the use of the drug nor the opium trade, but they refused to allow any government to forget the issue.

In the late nineteenth century opposition to the use of
opium was growing among diverse elements in both Brit-

ain and China. The medical profession, greatly aided by the China missionaries, was increasingly aware of the dangers of the use of opium in any form. The British government was increasingly plagued by the moral issue of the opium trade, which the missionaries were ever ready to point out. In China, many educated people were coming to view opium smoking as a curse, and they sought to end opium growth and consumption. Shortly after the turn of the century, all factors were right in both countries so that definite and determined steps could be taken to stop the use of the drug, which by then had few advocating its benefits, aside from those who earned their fortunes from its trade.

— THREE —
The Pro-Opium Forces
and Government Investigations

Denunciations of the opium trade did not deter it, as it continued throughout the nineteenth century and into the twentieth, in large part because many firms were involved in the business of dealing in opium and the government of India depended on the trade for some of its revenues and neither was willing to forgo the profits of the trade. There was also a demand for opium because of the number of Chinese who were addicted to it and, indeed, this demand was one of the arguments the pro-opium forces used to defend their position. The pro-opium forces argued if they did not sell opium to the Chinese, someone else would, and since they had long engaged in the business, it was logical they should continue to supply the Chinese market.

During these years, questions concerning the use of opium and the trade in the drug were investigated by both the British government and the United States government of the Philippines. Both appointed official commissions to study the problem, but there any similarity between the two investigations ends. The two commissions did their work ten years apart, the British in 1893-95 and the Americans in 1903-5, but their methods, purposes, and conclusions were separated by more than a decade. Appointed to appease the anti-opium party in Britain, the Royal Commission from the beginning was constituted and conducted itself in such a manner that its conclusions would support the pro-opium trade policies of the government. On the other side, the Philippine Commission was appointed to determine what the policy of the United States government toward the use of opium in the Philippines should be. Composed of only three people plus a secretary, it contrasted sharply to the larger Royal Commission with its nine members and numerous secretaries and assistants. The Americans traveled to all the places they wished to study so that they could gather firsthand evidence on which to base their conclusions. The British confined their investigations to London and India and never saw fit to visit China, which was the scene of the greatest amount of opium consumption.

THE INDIAN GOVERNMENT'S REVENUES

The question of revenue for the Indian government was a very important one, since part of its official income came from the production of opium on government lands and the taxes it collected from the sale and transportation of opium. At one time, approximately 16 percent of India's revenues were from opium.[1] Statistics on the actual amount of revenue the Indian government gained from opium were a matter of much dispute, owing partly to the problem of converting rupees into pounds sterling. The Indian government collected the largest sum from opium in the year 1880-81, when the amount was 8,451,382 tens of rupees. Of this figure, 5,926,924 tens of rupees were from the Bengal opium revenue and 2,524,458 tens of rupees were from the transit duty on opium. By 1892-93 the amount had declined to an estimated 5,399,800 tens of rupees, of which 3,571,000 tens of rupees were from Bengal and 1,747,000 tens of rupees from the transit taxes. Almost the whole of the Indian production of opium was exported to China and the Straits Settlement. The China trade reached its peak in 1879-80, when 94,835 chests were exported, and the Straits Settlement trade reached its peak in 1890-91, when 20,328 chests were exported. The average cost of a chest was 427 tens of rupees. Domestic consumption in India was listed at 6,320

chests in 1889-90,[2] while another account set the amount
for that year at 4,949 chests, only seven of which were used
for medicinal purposes.[3] The *Chinese Recorder* cited, in an
1893 editorial, the figure of £13 million as the estimated
annual value of the opium crop in India.[4] One unexpected
aspect of opium suppression in China in the early 1900s
was to send the demand for Indian opium skyrocketing. The
result was that instead of declining, the revenues of the Indian government increased by about 25 percent during that
period.[5]

Those who said the Indian government would stand to
lose too much of its income from the stoppage of the opium
traffic failed to consider that the lands used for the production of opium could quickly be converted to produce other
crops that the government might tax to make up the lost
revenue. If the government needed to compensate for the
lost revenues, the editors of the *Chinese Recorder* suggested,
they might tax luxury imports and curtail expensive public
works, huge civil bureaucracies, and the "needlessly elaborate military occupation." They also suggested that the pay
of European officials in India was exorbitant and that it was
improper for the British government to tax Hindus to support the Church of England when, officially, the government of India had no religion.[6] The extravagances of the
Indian government were also sharply criticized by Robert
Brown, who pointed out that the salaries of the India Office personnel in London surpassed the total income the
government gained from opium.[7]

THE PRO-OPIUM ADVOCATES

Pro-opium advocates vigorously supported the official
opium trade of the British government of India, and their
arguments were aimed at discrediting the views of the anti-
opium forces, as well as demonstrating that opium was a
harmless drug that the Indian government needed to mo-

nopolize in order to gain revenues it needed to function. While anti-opium advocates were largely clergymen, missionaries, and missionary doctors, the pro-opium forces included opium merchants, employees of the British colonial governments, and military men, particularly doctors.

Of the British firms trading in China, most were involved in the opium business. Jardine, Matheson and Company had engaged in the trade since the early years of the nineteenth century, when the founders of the company sold opium illegally along the China coast. Others, such as Dent and Company, were also active in the opium trade. A few European firms imported opium directly from India to China, but it was much more common for the opium trade from India to be in the hands of Indian firms, many of them controlled by Parsees. The most prominent of the firms trading in opium were those of the Sassoon family, who were thought to be Sephardic Jews.[8] The Sassoons' companies handled a variety of goods, but huge, quick profits attracted them to opium from time to time, particularly if they were in need of ready cash, and the family made the greater part of their fortune in opium.

A few of the Western business houses disliked trading in opium, especially as the moral issues came more and more to dominate the arguments for stopping the trade. Some firms, such as the Rathbones and the Holts, preferred not to engage in the opium trade but found that it was extremely difficult to free themselves of it completely. Even if they did not directly engage in the trade, from time to time they found it necessary to store their goods in warehouses that were also holding opium, or they had to rely on the opium-trading firms for business transactions. Eventually, the Rathbones abandoned their trading house in Canton because they found it impossible to disassociate themselves completely from the opium trade.[9] In the period prior to the Opium War, one American firm, Olyphant and Company of New York, run by D.W.C. Olyphant and his nephew,

Charles W. King, had refused to engage in the opium business as they considered the trade evil.[10] All Americans were
finally prohibited from engaging in the opium trade in
China in 1880, with the conclusion of a new Sino-Ameri-
can commercial treaty.

The pro-opium forces in Britain were quite vocal and
often used public debates to express their views on the question. One such meeting was held at the Royal Society of the
Arts in 1892. The pro-opium forces dominated the meeting, which centered around a paper presented by G.H.M.
Batten, formerly of the Bengal Civil Service. The paper and
responses to it were later published in the *Journal* of the
Society. Batten and other speakers defended the position
of the Indian government vis-à-vis opium and sharply attacked the China missionaries and others who sought to
abolish the trade.

Batten told the meeting "the indulgers in the drug have
been led to the habit by painful diseases, from which they
have sought and found relief in opium, and that these diseases—not due but antecedent to the resort to the drug—
largely account for the wretched appearance and condition
of the patients." He quoted a well-known pro-opium leader,
William H. Brereton, as saying "that opium smoking as practiced by the Chinese is perfectly innocuous, and that this is
a fact so patent that it forces itself upon the attention of
every intelligent resident in China who has given ordinary
attention to the subject." Concerning the China missionaries, Batten argued, "They are filled with a burning zeal to
better the physical and spiritual condition of the poor mis-
erable Chinese with whom they are brought into contact."
When the missionaries were met by Chinese "with the argument that opium is an evil thing, and that the English
who import it into China are out of Court when advocating morality, they fall into the trap, and jump to the conclusion that it is the opium trade which prevents their
making faster progress in the evangelization of China." He

concluded that the missionaries and the Society for the Suppression of the Opium Trade might convince the British government to end the trade and suppress the cultivation of the poppy and smuggling in India, but "you will never persuade the Chinese to follow in your footsteps, and abandon the ever-increasing culture of the poppy. . . . You will fail in any way to benefit China, unless you count it a benefit greatly to extend the cultivation of the poppy, and the manufacture of opium within her borders."[11]

The pro-opium advocates were fond of citing the case of the one China missionary who was among those opposing the request that Britain end the opium trade. In the early 1880s the Rev. F. Galpin of the English Methodist Free Church at Ningpo refused to sign a petition to the House of Commons asking for an end to the opium trade, saying he did not believe the "Chinese people or Government are really anxious to remove the abuse of opium. The remedy has always been, as it is now, in their own hands. Neither do I believe that if the importation of Indian opium ceased at once, the Chinese Government would set about destroying a very fruitful means of revenue. On the contrary, I feel sure that the growth of Chinese opium would be increased forthwith."[12]

Joseph G. Alexander was present at the meeting and, in a response following the presentation of Batten's paper, said the opposition of the Reverend Galpin was the only case of a missionary in China supporting the continuance of the opium trade. The rest of the missionaries were agreed that opium was an "unmitigated curse to the Chinese." Alexander was challenged by the pro-opium advocates to explain why only the Protestant missionaries were active in the anti-opium movement. His reply was that Henry Edward Cardinal Manning had said that Roman Catholic missionaries gave the same evidence as to the effects of opium smoking as did the Protestants.[13]

The opinions of several medical men were offered at the

meeting. One was quoted as having written, "I do not wish to defend the practice of opium smoking, but in the face of rash opinions and exaggerated statements . . . it is only right to record that no China resident believes in the terrible frequency of the dull, sodden-witted, debilitated opium smoker met with in print." He also stated that he had not found "many Europeans who believe that they ever get the better of their opium smoking compradores in the matter of business." Another medical doctor, who had been a first assistant opium examiner for the Indian government and who had spent three years in China, said, "The effects of the abuse of the drug do not come very frequently under observation" and that those that did occur were the result of taking the drug to cure an illness. "As regards the effects of the habitual use of the drug on the mass of the people, I must affirm that no injurious results are visible," he wrote. He concluded that opium use was no more pernicious than alcohol.[14]

Batten derided the idea, proposed by the Society for the Suppression of the Opium Trade, that domestic cultivation of the poppy in China be curtailed as the importation decreased. He noted that the Chinese government had had opium prohibition edicts for centuries and was unwilling or unable to enforce them. He could not imagine the Chinese government forgoing the customs revenues, which he set at £2 million a year and thought that any request to the Chinese that they curtail domestic production of opium would be met by laughter.[15]

Among those responding to Batten's paper was Sir Thomas Wade, who had spent some forty years in China and was appointed British minister to China in 1871. Wade said his information had been obtained in interviews with Chinese officials in the 1880s. The officials admitted the impossibility of abolishing opium smoking entirely but said if it could be accomplished, the Chinese government was willing to forgo its revenues from the trade. Wade acknowledged that any serious attempt to suppress the opium trade had to originate with the smokers. As long as addicts continued to smoke and wanted to smoke, the prohibition of the opium trade would be very difficult. He also said he believed opium reform would not come until the British sent to China men of education to convince the Chinese literati to end the use of opium.[16]

One of the outstanding pro-opium advocates, Sir Lepel Griffin, addressed the meeting, saying, "It was an astonishingly sad thing to see, in the latter part of the nineteenth century, a Society possessed of such mischievous, homicidal characteristics as the Anti-Opium Society. If their convictions were to prevail, they would rank as destroyers of the human race with cholera and famine, because a very large part of the population of India . . . was only preserved from death by the habitual use of opium." He ended by saying everyone of authority at the meeting knew that what he said was true.[17]

The meeting was long and heated and ended before everyone had had a chance to speak. In the published responses to Batten's paper, Sir John Strachey stated, "There can be no greater delusion than to suppose that China depends on India for her supply of opium. If no opium were exported from India, the consumption of China would remain practically unchanged. Indian opium in China is a luxury of the comparatively rich." He argued that since a single province of China produced more opium than the whole of India, it was not for the British to reproach themselves if the Chinese wanted to smoke opium and concluded that it would be "an act of folly and injustice" to deprive the Indian government of its opium revenues. Maurice Gregory, editor of Bombay's *Banner of Asia*, opposed the pro-opium speakers and cited the medical evidence of the dangers of abusing opium. Gregory wrote, "The fact should

be emphasized that the opium prepared by the British government in India is almost entirely used for purposes of
debauch."[18]

Few Britons ever publicly acknowledged using opium, but
one who did was Surgeon-General Sir William Moore. In
comments to the Royal Society, he said he had sought to
determine if opium was "the very injurious agent which it
has been asserted to be." In doing so, he spent twenty-five
years studying the question "among habitual opium consumers, and on the principle of experimenting on the vile
body I have used opium myself. I confidently assert that
opium is not the deadly agent which it has been painted;
and that climate, creed, habits, and customs render it almost a necessity for Eastern races." He went on to state that
opium alkaloids were poisonous, as were the alkaloids of
tea and coffee, but "no organic disease is caused by opium."
He suggested that the anti-opium forces could better use
their energies to eliminate the abuses of alcohol in Britain.
He continued that if the anti-opium forces succeeded in
abolishing the opium trade, the Indians would be worse off,
for without opium "the person suffering from want of food
would not be able to appease the hungry edge of appetite,"
and when famines occurred, thousands more would die, and
"the person having to undergo great physical fatigue would
not be able to render himself proof against it by opium,
neither would he be able to share the opium with his camel
or horse, which . . . was a point of honor with the riders."
He concluded that opium was "a safeguard against
malarious fevers, which could not be done if a physician's
prescription were required, for there is not a competent
doctor in every Indian village," and he thought that if opium
were prohibited the Indians would take to using Indian
hemp, "which was more injurious."[19]

E.L. Oxenham, a former British consul in China, commented that opium was a prophylactic against fever and was
widely used as such in the Yangtze valley and in Taiwan,

since quinine was prohibitively expensive. The use of opium in other areas, he believed, was abuse. He knew that the opium trade had been denounced by the Chinese government, the literati, and Buddhist and Taoist priests, but suppressing even half the cultivation of the poppy and the opium trade would require "measures, tyrannical and bloody in a high degree."[20]

Dr. James L. Maxwell brought up the fact that the Indian government refused to permit unlimited cultivation of the opium poppy and said that was "*prima facie* evidence that it recognizes its hurtful and demoralizing power." He cautioned that there were grave dangers in using the drug, except for medical purposes, and noted that the Indian government was aware of these dangers. He said the position of the government was self-contradictory; it prohibited the free cultivation of the poppy in India because of the dangers of the drug yet allowed the drug to be exported to China in great quantities. He questioned why the trade was allowed to continue when the dangers of the drug were well known. He wrote, "Since Englishmen have come into close contact with the Chinese, the universal testimony, even of the smokers themselves, has been that the habit is, physically and morally, degrading."[21]

Batten concluded the meeting by summing up that "in both China and India the moderate consumption of opium, even taken daily, is not only harmless but beneficial." He said that most consumers in both countries were moderate users and that "abuse or excessive use of opium is injurious, though not to the extent asserted by the Society for the Suppression of the Opium Trade, but the cases are exceptional, and cannot justify the destruction of a trade, the benefits of which far outweigh the evils."[22]

Anti-opium advocates sometimes found themselves at meetings or debates that were strongly in favor of the government's opium policy, as had happened to Joseph G. Alexander at the meeting of the Royal Society of the Arts

in 1892. The Rev. Montagu P. Beauchamp of the China Inland Mission found himself in a similar situation when he
was invited to a debate on opium in 1900 and discovered
the speakers were "almost to a man speaking in favor of
opium." Writing in the *Friend of China*, Beauchamp noted
that the pro-opium forces' major argument had previously
been that the government of India depended on the money
from the trade, but now he found "the constant cry . . .
'Oh, but opium is such a good thing for the native, and its
evils have been exaggerated.'" The speakers also mentioned
"the oft-used argument that there can be no harm in *moderate opium smoking*" and made the "fatal mistake" of comparing opium use in China to the alcohol problem in Britain.[23]

Speakers at the meeting included a former inspector of
prisons in Hong Kong who asserted that the opium habit
was easy to break, since anyone confined to jail had to give
it up immediately, and a businessman who insisted he had
never been inconvenienced by employees who were opium
smokers. Beauchamp learned after the meeting that the
"leader of the debate in favor of opium . . . had made every
dollar he possessed in the opium trade."[24]

Britishers who had lived in India were numerous among
the vocal pro-opium advocates. One refuted the charge that
opium produced insanity by stating that "in large doses [it]
produces hallucinations for a short time, but never insanity
in any form," and another stated that his banker was an
opium eater and "one of the shrewdest men of business in
all India." A planter who said he had been an "amateur
doctor" for many years in India stated that quinine was un-
suitable for many Indians, while opium was not. Sir William Roberts, a physician who served on the Royal Commission on Opium, insisted that opium could not be linked
to suicide since Assam, with the largest consumption of
opium, had the smallest number of suicides, and the province with the lowest consumption of opium, Madras, was
second among the provinces in the number of suicides.[25]

One of the charges made by those who opposed opium was that the British had forced opium on the Chinese and continued to do so under the treaties. These charges were refuted by many who supported the opium trade of the Indian government. Among those refuting the charge was Hartmann Henry Sultzberger who published a work, *All About Opium*, in 1884 that included a section, "The Forcing of Opium on the Chinese An Absolute Impossibility." Sultzberger argued that since the trade was agreed to by treaty it was not forced on the Chinese. Whether the treaty was "entered into in a purely commercial way, or obtained as a result of a successful war, does not affect the argument." He knew that the Chinese could not be forced to purchase opium, because in the previous two years he had attempted to sell three different qualities of opium in Hong Kong. One he sold at a modest profit and it was reordered, one "had to be sacrificed at a heavy loss," and the third could not be sold at all. He stated that the Chinese preferred the imported varieties of opium but that two-thirds to three-fourths of the opium used in China was domestically produced. He insisted the Chinese wanted to monopolize the entire business and found in the missionary "that rare combination of *'a readily believing and politically perfectly* irresponsible tool,' necessary for such an attempt." He did not want to accuse the Chinese and the missionaries of "having actually entered into . . . a compact," but he felt sure the "mere holding out to the worthy missionary of even the faintest of vain hopes in connection with his christianizing work . . . will at any time be quite sufficient to set him to work at once also at home, rendering him completely blind though, with respect to the damaging effects of this hopeless but persistent anti-opium agitation."[26]

Sultzberger was not alone in thinking the anti-opium forces were naive and the Chinese wanted to monopolize the trade. H.H. Kane in his account, *Opium-Smoking in America and China*, challenged the portrayal of the decline of a man who smoked opium in Broomhall's *The Chinese Opium Smoker*, saying he had met men who had been "hard smokers for ten years, and who present none of the features usually ascribed to the smoker."[27] And William H. Brereton, an adviser to an opium farmer, spoke for many of the pro-opium advocates when he said, "If the Chinese government really wanted to put a stop to [the trade] or check the use of opium they would begin by doing so themselves. They would first stop the cultivation of the drug in their own country." Brereton was sure the Chinese would not end opium use because of the large revenue they obtained from it.[28]

Other reasons were given for the Chinese desire to stop the trade. W.J. Moore wrote that in their protests the Chinese had not been honest: "the real reason they [do] not desire the trade [is] . . . *first* the fear of the great exportation of silver; and *secondly*, a stinging sense of humiliation from being obliged, as the result of British victories, to admit Indian opium to the treaty ports on a fixed tariff."[29]

In 1903 some members of the House of Commons expressed their belief that if India were to stop exporting opium to China the Chinese would increase domestic production, so that within a few years they would not only fulfill their own needs, but would also be exporting the drug to fill the needs of other countries.[30] The pro-opium advocates were staunch in their conviction that opium was harmless and that, hence, there was no need to end the official opium trade. They attributed to the Chinese the desire to end the Indian opium trade so that they might increase domestic production and monopolize the opium business for themselves. There was a distinct difference between those who advocated the continuance of the opium trade and those who favored its abolition, however. For the most part, those advocating the continuation of the trade were either opium planters or sellers or officials of the British Indian government. Some medical doctors did argue that opium was harmless, but they, too, tended to be employees of the Indian government or officers of the British army in India. In contrast, the majority of those who opposed opium were more familiar with China, and they tended to be missionaries or missionary doctors who had no direct or personal interest in the policies of the Indian government. Certainly, individuals who made their livings from the opium trade had a vested interest in the continuation of that trade.

The pro-opium advocates were frequent in their comparisons of opium to alcohol, although they were not alone in these comparisons. Some argued that if opium were no more harmful than alcohol, then if one wished to abolish the opium trade, one also should wish to abolish the trade in alcoholic beverages.

The extremes to which the pro-opium advocates went to defend their position is evident by the statement of Surgeon-General Sir William Moore, who said opium was a necessity because it was useful to assuage the appetite in time of famine. He apparently chose not to consider that food could be used for the same purpose!

Some of the medical men who called opium harmless might be excused for their statements because of the general lack of information on the subject of addiction. In the late nineteenth century the most accurate information on opium addiction was being compiled by the missionary doctors in China, and their evidence often tended to be discounted by doctors employed by the British government in India, not so much on medical grounds, but rather, on the basis that the government doctors favored the government's policy on opium, while the missionary doctors did not.

THE ROYAL COMMISSION ON OPIUM

As the British government became increasingly pressured by the anti-opium forces, which were harder and harder to ignore, it finally decided to appoint a commission to investigate the use of opium and the involvement of the Indian government in the opium trade. The Royal Commission on Opium, appointed in June 1893, was to study the question and report what changes could be made in the military and civil expenditures of India, by what means India's resources could be developed, and what temporary assistance the government would need to compensate for suppressing the opium traffic.[31]

Opposition to the appointment of a commission was intense and the secretary of state for India, the earl of Kimberley, declared he would resign rather than consent to a resolution that suggested that the opium revenue in India might be surrendered. Prime Minister William Gladstone, who as a young man had been strongly opposed to the opium trade, proposed the resolution on behalf of the government, calling for a royal commission to report on the issue. The Commission was to consider prohibiting the growth of poppies and the sale of opium except for medical purposes, the arrangements the British had with the Native States regarding shipments of opium, what effect stopping the trade would have on the finances of India, whether any change of policy short of complete prohibition was a possibility, consumption of opium patterns by different groups of people in India and the moral and physical effects such use had, and the willingness of the Indian people to give up non-medical uses of opium and their willingness to bear the costs of prohibition.[32] The vote on Gladstone's resolution was 184 for and 105 against, with the anti-opium M.P.s voting against the measure on the grounds that it did not deal with the Chinese aspect of the opium trade.[33]

The Commission was composed of nine members: Lord Brassey, chairman; two officials of the Indian government, Sir James B. Lyall and Arthur N. Fanshawe, director-general of the Post Office of India; two Indians, Sir Lachhmesswar Singh Bahadur, maharaja of Barbhanga, and Haridas Veharidas, former dewan (prime minister) of

Junagarh; two anti-opium representatives Arthur Pease and Henry J. Wilson, a Liberal M.P.; an independent medical man, Sir William Roberts, M.D.; and an independent member of Parliament, Robert G. C. Mowbray, a Conservative. The secretary of the Commission was J. Prescott Hewett.[34]

In China, the *Chinese Recorder* greeted the news of the appointment of the Royal Commission with an editorial saying, "We rejoice with and congratulate the home anti-opium crusaders who accept the decision of the House of Commons as the greatest and most solid forward step that the movement for the suppression of the opium trade has yet made."[35] But Li Hung-chang, upon hearing that the British government had appointed the Royal Commission on Opium, was reported to have remarked that it was absurd to appoint a commission to inquire if opium were harmful since "everybody knows that opium is most injurious."[36]

The Commission met for a week in September in London where it took evidence from a number of officials who had had experience in India and other British possessions in Asia. Then it moved to India, where it heard persons from India and Burma and other parts of Asia from 18 November 1893 to 22 February 1894. They also sent questionnaires to the British Consuls in China and the colonial authorities in Hong Kong and the Straits Settlement, asking that they be given to "the most intelligent and trustworthy gentlemen of Oriental races, and officials, medical men, merchants, and others, who are specially conversant with Chinese and other Asiatic consumers of opium."[37]

Because royal commissions were appointed by the Crown or Parliament, they were generally thought to be unbiased and to conduct "objective enquiries systematically planned by unbiased persons of great intelligence who were only anxious to find out the truth. There were often anything but that." Certainly the Royal Commission on Opium fit this description. The anti-opium leaders were unhappy with the appointment of the Commission since it was not going to investigate, specifically, the question of the opium trade and its effects on China. Like many official commissions and committees it was "carefully organized by those who promoted [it] to drive home a particular point of view, [and] to support one side in a controversy." Such committees had members who "were chosen, the evidence carefully selected and the proceedings marshalled so that the desired conclusions could be embodied in a report, which could be . . . a most effective instrument for the control of opinion."[38] Yet once the Royal Commission on Opium was named, the Society for the Suppression of the Opium Trade, as well as the other anti-opium groups, had to make the best of the situation.

In hopes of influencing the Commission to favor ending the opium trade, representatives of various anti-opium groups in London issued an appeal to the Commission that the truth on opium be brought out, while at the same time explaining their position with regard to the Commission. They stated that they did not desire the appointment of the Commission since the use of the drug in India was "a comparatively small though important portion of the moral iniquity, as it does not form one-twelfth of the India Opium Trade." They said they were more concerned with the fact that "a nominally Christian Government" obtained revenue from the manufacture and commerce in the drug that was so harmful to the people of China and the Straits Settlement. They pointed out that if the majority of the people in Britain wanted to end the Indian opium traffic there was no need to appoint a commission but rather the need to seek a different source of revenue for the Indian government.[39]

The statement pointed out that the anti-opium societies did not have the funds to send expensive telegrams "in correction of the one-sided reports from India day by day—nor have they the resources at their command which in other ways are available by the Indian Government, the uphold-ers of the Opium Traffic." They noted that Joseph G. Alexander, secretary of the Society for the Suppression of the Opium Trade, had gone to India at his own expense to aid the Commission in its investigation. He found it impossible to do so alone, so had secured the assistance of the Rev. Thomas Evans, a missionary who had had thirty-eight years of experience in India. The statement appealed for £2,000 immediately, £1,000 to go to Alexander in India and another £1,000 to be divided between the Society for the Suppression of the Opium Trade, the Urgency Committee, and the Women's Urgency Committee. In an appeal that accompanied the statement they noted that there was "undue prominence" being given in the press to "those who declare the use of Opium, other than medicinally, to be harmless, and even beneficial to health, without publishing the strong evidence given against the illegitimate use of the drug." As an example, they cited an item from the *Newcastle Daily Chronicle* that said they would be surprised if the result of the Commission's investigation were "not to increase the consumption of the drug in the Western world, where it has hitherto been used very little, if at all. All the credible evidence tends to show that those who do not use Opium are losers by their abstinence." There was also the statement of a medical doctor who insisted that in thirty-eight years of practice he had "never found Opium to be deleterious to health, but to the contrary, considered that it increases longevity. Opium eaters . . . are generally healthy men, and contrast favorably with non-Opium eaters." The anti-opium leaders feared that as a result of such statements more people would be brought "under the terrible slavery of the evil habit." They cited the statement of thousands of missionaries and doctors in India, China, and Britain as evidence of the dangerous effects of opium.[40]

Yet, despite the alarm of some of the anti-opium forces, many still thought the Commission would explore all sides of the question fairly. An editorial in the *Chinese Recorder* in

January 1894 quoted the *Friend of China* as saying, "All that we have seen of these members of the Commission who have attended its sittings in London and all that we hear of the two native members of the Commission, leads us to believe that the Commission is as fair-minded and impartial a tribunal as we could have desired to hear our case." The *Chinese Recorder* noted that the British government had at last been compelled to investigate the matter and expressed the belief that a long step had been taken, even though it was acknowledged that it was too much to hope "that British connection with the opium traffic with China will be broken immediately."[41]

In India the selection of witnesses for the Commission was done by representatives of the Indian government. They were quite aware of the position of the British government regarding the opium trade and wished to supply witnesses who would support the government's position. Accordingly, some "acted unscrupulously in the selection of witnesses; . . . when everyone knows what kind of evidence an omnipotent government wants, only a very brave man, especially of the conquered people, will, in open session, give evidence opposed to the wishes of his rulers."[42]

Once it became evident to the missionaries in China that the Commission would confine its work to Britain and India and not visit China, some questioned whether the Commission could fully investigate the opium problem. Some farsighted missionaries concluded that the final report of the Commission would not contribute to ending the opium trade, which was the desire of both the China missionaries and the anti-opium societies.

The Royal Commission's work on China consisted of sending questions regarding opium consumption and revenues to the British consuls in China. Along with the twenty-four witnesses from China who had testified in London and the ten who testified in India, there were a total of 178 persons who offered evidence from China. These included thirty-four consuls, sixteen Chinese, forty-seven medical doctors (including missionary doctors), thirty-seven merchants, and forty-four missionaries.[43]

The difficulty of obtaining information from consuls was well expressed by Consul Everard H. Fraser, who said there was only one merchant in his area and he was a German who had nothing to do with the opium trade, which was largely in the hands of Chinese. Several of the consuls expressed the thoughts of Consul Scott, who said the missionaries had the best information on the question of opium and his own observations were mostly secondhand since he had never studied the question of opium addiction among the Chinese. Consul T.L. Bullock wrote, "The papers are for the most part furnished by missionaries. But missionaries in China, speaking the language, constantly moving about, and always in close contact with the people, are able to give far more trustworthy opinions on such a subject than any other class of persons can, though many of them, of course, have strong prejudices concerning [opium]." Consul Clement F.R. Allen wrote, "As a private resident in China my experiences in China have not the weight either of those of a medical man or those of a missionary. We Consuls have little private intercourse with the natives outside our homes and offices." Consul Byron Brenan reported that a Chinese general told him that "the pseudo pleasure [of opium] is obtained at the expense of natural contentment," and that farmers, "who work hard all year round [and] know too well the value of money," generally did not smoke opium.[44] Nearly all the consuls agreed that alcohol would not be used as a substitute for opium by the Chinese. On the question of why the British dealt in opium with the Chinese, Sir Thomas Wade, testifying before the Royal Commission, perhaps best summed up the situation when he said, "Our grand difficulty with China is that we never have anything to offer."[45]

Those witnesses from China who defended the opium

habit offered little positive evidence to suggest that the habit
really was beneficial. One even said, "It is no doubt a great
pity that the Chinese should be so addicted to opium." Another, who had been a large importer of the drug, argued,
"Being on demand, and so largely required, it must have
some beneficial effect." Another, who thought the missionaries had greatly exaggerated the harm opium wrought, still
wrote, "Burden coolies would be better and stronger men,
and able to endure as much work if they never commenced
the habit. . . . I think all native and foreign employers look
with a watchful and suspicious eye on the opium smoker."[46]

The consul at Shanghai gave the Commission's questions
to the Rev. Griffith John and some other missionaries at
Hankow for their responses. The replies of John were
printed in the *Chinese Recorder*. Among the questions[47] asked
were, "What were the observed moral, physical, and social
effects of opium upon its consumers?" and "Is the effect
the same on consumers of each race, or can you draw dis-
tinctions between the effects on consumers of different
races?" and "Is there any difference between the effects of
Indian and Chinese grown opium?" John replied, "The
moral effects of opium are of the most pernicious kind. . . .
Not only is the moral sense weakened in the opium victims,
but they are led by the habit into associations, where they
are directly tempted to the most profligate vices. The opium
dens are, for the most part, sinks of iniquity, and opium
smoking is generally associated with debauchery, gambling
and other gross vices." He reported that physically the drug
led to great injury and death. The Chinese recognized the
effect of opium on reproduction and "affirm[ed] that the
family of the opium smoker will be extinct in the third gen-
eration." The social effects, he said, were "impoverishment,"
"untrustworthiness," and "lazy habits." Concerning the different effects on the different races, he said, "The effects
are the same on all the Chinese with whom I have had to
do." He compared Indian opium to Chinese opium by say-

ing the former was much stronger and was like comparing a coal fire to a fire of wood. Indian opium was "more expensive and beyond the reach of the poorer classes," but he noted that the native product was used to adulterate the foreign drug.

Another question concerned what would happen if the supply of the drug from India were cut off. John replied that addicts would use the Chinese-produced drug unless the Chinese government could take some action to stop its growth.[48] On this question others were also skeptical that stopping the traffic from India would change things in China. The former governor of Hong Kong, G. W. Des Voeux, in a letter to the Royal Commission, said that even if the Commission succeeded in stopping the Indian opium trade, this would not alter patterns of consumption in China. He noted that Indian opium was "regarded as superior in flavor, [and was] used in China as a luxury of the comparatively rich."[49] He continued that if the trade were stopped, the Chinese would use the native product, but he also believed that smuggling of Indian opium would increase dramatically. He suggested that the inhabitants of Hong Kong were the heaviest consumers of opium in the world and attributed this to the comparatively high pay earned by Hong Kong residents, which meant they could afford the drug. According to his estimate, the amount of opium sold by the local opium monopoly equalled the amount estimated to be smuggled into the colony from the mainland. He questioned why the missionaries were so concerned with the opium trade when it was not the British or other Europeans, but "the Parsees, Armenians, Hebrews, and others who have been brought up and educated in the East" who controlled the trade almost exclusively. He suggested that the missionaries' motive was to have a vivid issue with which to attract money for their China missions.[50]

Another of the Commission's questions was, "Do people of European race contract the opium habit in any numbers?

If not, why not? And what makes Asiatics more liable to contract the habit?" John's reply was, "Very rarely. During my long residence in China I have met with only two cases. The phlegmatic temperament and indolent habits of the Asiatic make him more liable to contract the habit." Responding to why the Chinese used opium, John listed first "the love of pleasure and vice. The opium dens are moral sinks, and opium smoking is associated with gambling and gross sensual indulgence." Second, he mentioned the use of opium to cure physical ailments or relieve pain; third, "it is supposed to facilitate business transactions and the striking of bargains"; and, fourth, he suggested "indolence and the want of occupation." He discounted its use as a prophylactic.[51]

In response to a question asking if the Chinese desired that England end the opium trade, John wrote, "There is decidedly a wish that the foreign importation should be discontinued. The people generally look upon the opium vice as having been introduced by foreigners, without distinguishing between one nation and another, and they look upon its introduction as an immoral and hostile act." He continued that "the relation between the two countries can never be what it ought to be whilst this traffic lasts, and that the moral effect of its abandonment by England on the Chinese mind would be very powerful and highly favorable. The Chinese as a people would begin to see us in a new light and feel towards us as they have never done hitherto."[52]

In conclusion, John said that he was unable to say what the Chinese government might do if the importation of opium from India were stopped, but he thought the government would make "an honest effort to stop the native growth, and the attempt *might* eventuate the diminution of the evil, if not its complete suppression." He could see "no hope for the *speedy* deliverance of China from the vice" if the trade continued. He wrote, "The evil is now one of enor-

mous magnitude, and the venality of the officials is as deep
rooted as ever, and I therefore fear that no legislative measures on the part of the Central government, however hon-
estly adopted, would put an end to opium smoking, and
consequently to opium growth in China itself." John noted,
however, that there were others who disagreed with him on
the subject. He did say that whatever the Chinese government did "the path of England, as a great Christian nation,
seems to me to be perfectly clear. It is for us to wash our
hands clean of the trade which is unworthy of ourselves and
hurtful to the people of China." John said that opium was
becoming a very common means of committing suicide and
concluded that "opium in China is an awful curse, and that
in more ways than one."[53]

Perhaps one of the most unexpected witnesses before the
Commission was the merchant, Donald Matheson, who had
resided in China for ten years while a partner in Jardine,
Matheson and Company, which had long engaged in the
opium traffic. Matheson was active in the anti-opium movement in Britain, and now he publicly told the Commission
he favored an end to the opium trade from which many of
his relatives made their livings.[54]

While the Commission was sitting, the pages of the *Chinese Recorder* were rich with comments about its work. The
Rev. Henry Woods in a letter to the editor criticized the
secular press for "industriously presenting the side of the
question favorable to opium" and denouncing "those who
know the facts and tell the truth about opium." He suggested
the *Chinese Recorder* publish a symposium on the observations of the missionaries concerning opium, but he noted
that such testimonies "might be branded as *lies* by the opposite side who must rely mainly on discourteous epithets
to uphold their side of the question."[55]

The missionaries in China recognized the importance of
having their views presented to the Royal Commission. Accordingly, British missionaries who had had at least twenty-

five years of service in China joined in a memorial to the
Commission. The points made in the memorial were: that
it had been established "beyond possibility of reasonable
doubt that the consumption of opium in China is exerting
a distinctly deteriorating effect upon the Chinese people,
physically, socially, and morally"; that the Chinese people
were "as a whole distinctly opposed to the opium habit";
that although the opium trade was no longer illegal, it was
"highly injurious, not only to China but also to the fair name
of Great Britain"; and that the opium imported to China
from India was not for medical purposes nor used as such,
and "hence we regard the importation as being wholly preju-
dicial to the well being of the Chinese people." The missionaries asked that the Commission recommend opium
production in India be limited to that needed for medicinal purposes in India and elsewhere. They noted that testimony had been given that stated that "the consumption of
opium by the peoples of India is not accompanied with the
same disastrous consequences that we have all witnessed for
ourselves in China. . . . We are of the opinion that a longer
and wider range of experience will certainly show that
opium is as injurious *to all other races* as it has been proved
to be to the Chinese." They noted that England classed
opium as a dangerous poison, as did other countries, and
concluded, "We cannot believe that what is a dangerous
poison to the greater part of the human race acts only as a
harmless stimulant on other parts of the race."[56]

The report of the Royal Commission was presented to
Parliament on 26 April 1895. On the subject of opium smoking in China the majority report concluded, "By the majority of the missionaries of every Christian communion,
the use of opium is strongly condemned." Among those in
the British consular service, "the prevailing opinion is that
opium smoking in moderation is not harmful, and that
moderation is the rule. The evil effects of excess do not

thrust themselves prominently on the notice. A minority of
the Consular service condemn the use of opium in any form
as essentially bad. The medical opinions were in general
accord with those of the consular body." Accordingly, the
Commission thought "that the habit is generally practiced
in moderation, and that when so practiced the injurious
effects are not apparent; but that, when the habit is carried
to excess, disastrous consequences, both moral and physical, inevitably follow. We may fairly compare the effects of
opium smoking among the Chinese population to those of
alcoholic liquors in the United Kingdom."[57] The report went
on to say that the Chinese were "a perfectly free agent" with
regard to opium and that there was "no evidence from China
of any popular desire that the import of Indian opium
should be stopped."[58]

THE MISSIONARIES REFUTE THE ROYAL COMMISSION'S REPORT

The issuance of the Royal Commission's report produced
much criticism by those who thought the Commission's work
had been unfairly conducted because the views of dissent-
ing members were not given widespread publicity. The anti-
opium forces were quick to produce evidence they said refuted the conclusions of the Commission, and indeed they
used the evidence presented to the Commission to illustrate
that its conclusions were contradictory to its own evidence.

In India the Commission examined 722 witnesses, including 55 native medical men, 74 European officials, 47 missionaries, 89 officials of native states, and 57 landowners.
The report issued by the Commission consisted of five volumes and supplements, without indexes, and with no order to the arrangement of the evidence. Joshua Rowntree
undertook to present a systematic review of the evidence
in his work *The Opium Habit in the East: A Study of the Evidence Given to the Royal Commission on Opium, 1893-94* but

Upper-class woman and man smoking opium, most likely
in their own home, probably in Peking. Library of
Congress.

noted in his introductory remarks that the "present dura-
tion of human life is hardly sufficient to allow of many persons reading through these five volumes."[59]

Rowntree concluded about the Commission's work that
the government ministers had given erroneous information
on opium to the Parliament. As evidence of this he cited
the statement that the government of India sought to diminish the area of poppy cultivation in India and the statement that China was free to terminate the opium trade on
its own. "Both of these statements were made and confirmed
by responsible statesmen in their official capacities, and both
are shown beyond all gain-saying to be misstatements of the
actual facts," he wrote. Regarding the results of the
Commission's inquiry on the question of opium in China,
"poor and partial" as it was, Rowntree wrote, it "show[ed]
afresh . . . the disastrous consequences of the opium habit

in China; and point[ed] . . . with curious precision, to the
undermining of the fabric of that ancient State which is
every day becoming more and more apparent." With regard to China, Rowntree noted that the medical evidence
concerning the prophylactic properties of opium with reference to malaria directly contradicted those presented by
medical men in India, who insisted the drug was useful for
this purpose.[60]

In response to the question why Europeans did not become addicted to the drug, one person told the Commission that Europeans did not smoke opium because it required reclining on a couch and it was "uncomfortable to
lie down for any length of time wearing a pair of tight trou-
sers and ordinary boots." Others reported that Europeans
who used the drug became quite as addicted to it as did the
Chinese. One medical doctor reported that the Europeans
did not like to smoke opium because the habit would asso-
ciate them with Chinese tastes and they wished to avoid such
an association. Consul Bullock said the Europeans did not
take opium because if they did they would become "objects
of contempt, even to the least particular of their acquain-
tances." However, some witnesses noted that opium and
morphia addiction among Europeans was increasing. One
reported that in Tongking "among the French people, quite
a number have taken to opium, and it is becoming quite a
curse." This was confirmed by Consul Parker, who said the
French officials in Tongking had been "officially warned"
about the dangers of the drug.[61]

Opium had been a problem in Burma until the Burmese
requested that the Indian government prohibit the sale of
the drug there on the grounds that the Buddhism they practiced forbade them to use the drug. In March 1893 the government of India had worked out an agreement with the
Burmese to ban the use of opium in Lower Burma, as it
had previously done in Upper Burma. The official statement said, "The use of opium is condemned by the Bud-

dhist religion; and government, believing the condemnation to be right, intends that the use of opium by persons
of the Burmese race shall forever cease." Needless to say,
the China missionaries were greatly encouraged by this statement and they pointed it out to the Royal Commission.[62]

Testimony from the Straits Settlement was that "respect-
able Chinese merchants, shopkeepers, clerks and domes-
tics are in a marked degree indisposed to confess to any
opium smoking, or to admit opium smokers to their employment. Various explanations are given for this fact, but
it seems in any case to be firmly held as part of the recognized Chinese code of moral opinion." Although the government of the Straits Settlement monopolized opium, "any
employee of the opium farm in Singapore who is known to
smoke opium is at once dismissed," because addicts were
known to be untrustworthy. Hong Kong derived about one-
sixth of its revenue from opium, and 61 persons responded
to the questions sent to the colonial secretary there. They
included only two missionaries, one a medical doctor. Of
those responding to the questions, only one medical doctor
said that the opium habit was beneficial, and only one of
the eight Chinese responding defended the habit. One of
the Chinese, Lau Wai-chun, concluded his testimony by saying, "In thus stopping the supply of opium, the whole of
Asia will be benefited, and England will be carrying out
the will of Heaven in protecting its children, and will receive in return infinite blessings." Several persons told the
Commission that morphine was becoming a more serious
problem in the colony.[63]

In testimony concerning China, which accounted for the
consumption of nine-tenths of India's production of opium
but which occupied comparatively little of the Commission's
investigation, two questions were paramount. One was
whether Britain had forced opium upon the Chinese and
the other was whether or not China was now free to refuse
the importation of the drug. Sir Joseph W. Pease told the

Commission that when the English forced opium on China, they encouraged the domestic cultivation of the drug. Horatio Nelson Lay, who had helped the Chinese with naval matters earlier in the century, testified before the Commission that "the pretence that we have forced opium on the Chinese is fustian, and [the Chinese authorities] are only making those statements for the purpose of damaging the English." He also thought the Americans had inserted a clause in their commercial treaty with the Chinese making opium contraband "as a slap in the face of the English." He went on to say the Chinese "have encouraged our opium, and we, by *allowing the Chinese to overtax it,* have stimulated the growth of the native article enormously in every province. I think that the most short-sighted policy that ever was pursued on our part."[64]

The anti-opium leaders challenged the conclusions of the Royal Commission in a second major work, this one Arnold Foster's *Report of the Royal Commission on Opium Compared with the Evidence from China that was Submitted to the Commission: An Examination and An Appeal,* published in 1899. In his preface—which was signed by Frederick Temple, archbishop of Canterbury, six bishops of the Church of England, and 141 other prominent persons—Foster quoted from Chang Chih-tung's recently published work, *Learn,* on the evils of opium and challenged anyone to find a statement from a Chinese author in support of the opium habit. Foster also noted that the marquis of Salisbury had stated that the British policy toward China was "very simple. It is to maintain the Chinese Empire, to prevent it falling into ruins, to invite it into paths of reform, and to give it every assistance which we are able to give it, to perfect its defence or to increase its commercial prosperity. By so doing we shall be aiding its cause and our own."[65]

Foster noted that he used in the text of his book no antiopium evidence that had not been presented to the Royal Commission and said it was not his intention to explore the whole of the opium question or to write an anti-opium tract but rather only to examine the evidence before the Commission. That alone, he said, was enough to refute the conclusions of the Commission. Foster suggested that Britain could help the Chinese Empire "from falling into ruins" by abandoning the opium trade. "If England persists in refusing to recognize this evil, all other movements which she may make in the direction of reforming China will be found to be unavailing," he wrote. Foster's major thesis was that the evidence presented to the Commission directly conflicted with the conclusions the Commission drew from that evidence, and he systematically set out to prove his point. Two examples of such conclusions were "there is no evidence from China of any popular desire that the import of Indian opium should be stopped" and "in the British Consular service in China, the prevailing opinion is that opium smoking in moderation is not harmful, and that moderation is the rule. . . . The medical opinions were in general accord with those of the Consular body." Foster pointed out that the Commission had received a large amount of evidence from Chinese calling for the end of the importation of opium from India, and that the great majority of medical witnesses from China stated that moderation in the use of opium was rare and that opium was definitely harmful. Foster stated that such inaccuracies led him to have "grave suspicions as to the trustworthiness of the China Report as a whole."[66]

Foster noted that the Commission's report stated that it was not allowed to cross-examine witnesses on the moral and physical effects of the use of opium in China, yet its own report contained testimony from such witnesses whom they had cross-examined![67] He believed that a careful examination of the evidence would support the statement in the minority report of one of the Commissioners, Henry J. Wilson, who wrote, "The Report adopted by my colleagues appears to me to partake more of the character of an elaborate defence of the opium trade of the East India Company, and of the present Government of India, than of a judicial pronouncement on the immediate questions submitted to us." Foster criticized the Commission for gathering evidence on opium from Europeans, particularly European government officials in Asia. He said the opinions of the native peoples should be considered, and he lauded the efforts of Wilson along those lines. Wilson noted that there had been a change in the attitudes of government officials in recent years—that earlier all officials had condemned opium. He cited a letter from the directors of the East India Company to the governor general in 1817 that described opium as "a pernicious drug" and stated "were it possible to prevent the use of the drug altogether, except strictly for the purpose of medicine, we would gladly do it in compassion to mankind."[68]

Foster attacked the Commission's statement that "the effects of the use and abuse of opium in China are fairly comparable with those of intoxicating liquors in England" and its opinion that the moral objections were not sufficient to warrant stopping the trade. As long as the Chinese government allowed the importation of opium and was not intimidated or pressured into allowing the importation, the Commission saw no need for interference from the British government to stop the exportation of the drug from India. Foster pointed out that this justification for the Indian government's position failed to consider that great quantities of opium were being exported to Hong Kong and the Straits Settlement for use by people living under British rule. He also pointed out that the Commissioners had no recommendations for curtailing the consumption of opium in any British-ruled area.[69]

Foster said the argument that China would supply its own opium if the British did not was invalid. He said Sir Joseph Pease had succinctly dealt with that question on the day the Commission began its hearings when he quoted from

Dymond's "Essay on Morality," "'I have no right to do that which is wrong, if it is wrong, because somebody else is going to do wrong.' [This argument] I think has no defence in solid international morality." And Wilson, in his minutes of dissent, acknowledged that the Chinese grew opium, either with or without the permission of authorities, and no one could say what the Chinese would do to curtail domestic cultivation if the importation were stopped, "but however that may be, a traffic which is contrary to the principles of humanity cannot be justified on the ground that, if we do not engage in it, it will fall into the hands of others who have no such scruples." Foster noted that the Commissioners justified the continuation of the opium trade on the very grounds Pease and Wilson condemned it.[70]

In response to the Commission's statement that "there is no evidence from China of any popular desire that the import of Indian opium should be stopped," Foster quoted numerous people from China who urged the Commission to stop the trade. Among these was Yu King-pak, son of a yamen official at Canton, who said, "there is no room for empty excuses, let them make haste to help China and do away with this huge evil." Lu Pao-yu, who was employed by the British Consulate at Chefoo, wrote, "The inhabitants of Shantung naturally do not like England to import Indian opium. Every chest . . . is so much injury to the people, and the flood of poison is never ending." Similar comments were received from other Chinese, as well as from British government officials, missionaries, and missionary doctors. Foster also printed the memorial of the missionaries with twenty-five or more years of service in China and cited it as evidence that contradicted the conclusions of the Commission.[71]

He criticized the Commission for the use of such words as "use of opium," "moderate use," and "without injury"[72] and for the wording of its questionnaire, which was sent to the British minister in China for distribution to the con-

suls, because it contained no questions to ascertain if the
person replying were a disinterested party or even what his
standing was in China. To illustrate this lack, Foster cited
the testimony given by T.W. Duff, "a merchant in China of
thirty years' standing, whose opinion is 'that in the circumstance of their living, food, climate, and habitations, opium
has no deleterious effects upon the Chinese; indeed, quite
the contrary, for it is a positive need, and they could not do
without it.'" Although Duff gave evidence twice, once in
London and once from China, no one asked him his business, which Foster learned was opium importation.[73]

Foster quoted from the report, "Opium exported to
China and the Far East is thus far larger than that consumed
in India, to which it bears the proportion of about twelve
to one." He suggested if that were the case, then the Commission should have been concerned with China to a far
greater extent, since the harm there was "of twelve times
greater importance to the human race." Concerning the
views of the China missionaries, the report stated that the
Commission had taken evidence from seventeen missionaries who had resided in China and from Benjamin
Broomhall, general secretary of the China Inland Mission,
and, from their testimonies, had concluded, "the evidence
of these witnesses was practically unanimous as to the evil
effects of opium-smoking upon the Chinese, though that
of Dr. W. Lockhart, a medical missionary of the London
Missionary Society, was less pronounced than that of the
others."[74] Foster pointed out that the testimony the Commissioners had dispatched with that short statement had
come from the Rev. J. Hudson Taylor, the founder and di-
rector of the China Inland Mission; the Rev. James Legge,
professor of Chinese at Oxford, who had resided in China
for thirty-three years; and James L. Maxwell, M.D., who had
presented the Commission a memorial denouncing both the
use of opium and the opium trade, which had been signed
by five thousand medical men in Britain, ten of whom were

fellows of the Royal Society and thirty-five of whom had
practiced medicine in either India or China. Foster pointed
out that the Commission's statement made it appear that
Dr. Lockhart was the only medical missionary to give testimony and that his statements, which included the comment
that the opium smoker "becomes so deteriorated, and so
debased in every way, that [he is] not allowed to give evidence in any legal proceedings in any of the courts of justice in China," did not condemn the use of the drug. Foster
also noted that, of the seventeen missionaries who testified,
many gave evidence in the form of letters from other missionaries who were not able to appear before the Commission.[75]

Foster repeatedly illustrated that the Commission's report was based on statements taken out of context or partially quoted to support the pro-opium bias of the Commission. For example, the report stated, "By the majority of
the missionaries of every Christian community in China the
use of opium is strongly condemned." Yet the Commission
went on to quote at length two missionaries who dissented
from that opinion, and the testimony of one of them was
taken out of context in the report. The report stated that
the Rev. W. Ashmore of the American Baptist Mission, who
had served forty-three years in China, said "that some men
will use opium for years and show no marked results," yet
his whole statement, which appeared in the Commission's
volumes of evidence, was "some men of vigorous vitality
will use opium for many years and not show marked results. Others show the effects almost immediately in a general, physical, and moral deterioration."[76]

Foster also questioned the validity of the testimony of
the British consuls. Consul Allen of Chefoo stated that as a
private resident of China he had little opportunity to meet
with Chinese and hence did not know the extent of opium
use or the harm it might cause but that as a judge of the
Mixed Court at Shanghai he had seen many opium sots who
had become criminals.[77]

Concerning the opinion of medical men, the Commission listed ten private doctors and twelve government medical officers who gave testimony on opium and noted that eight of them said the effects of the use of opium were favorable, five said the effects were doubtful, and nine said they were unfavorable. Foster questioned why the report listed only these twenty-two medical doctors when forty had given testimony to the Commission. Of the eighteen whose opinions were omitted from the report's conclusions, all but one were unfavorable to the use of opium. The one opinion considered favorable was given by the only medical doctor testifying that opium was not frequently used to commit suicide in China.[78]

Chinese testifying before the Commission presented special problems, particularly with translation. Only two Chinese witnesses gave pro-opium testimony, and Foster suspected that in at least one case the statement attributed to a Chinese witness was actually the opinion of the pro-opium translator, since the Chinese man was quoted as having said that in China "some people regarded opium much as a strict Methodist in England would regard theatres or cards." Foster commented, "Much a Chinaman knows of what strict Methodists in England think of theatres and cards!"[79]

Foster categorized the missionaries' testimony as thirty-three unfavorable to opium, none favorable, and one doubtful. Of the Chinese, eight were unfavorable, two were favorable (including the one who remarked on "strict Methodists"), and one was doubtful. Merchants also gave testimony to the Commission, although no attempt was made to ascertain if they had any interests in the opium trade. Of the twenty-six merchants giving testimony, Foster was only able to determine that six, including the representatives of Jardine, Matheson and Company, the Sassoons, and T.W. Duff, were involved in the opium business. Five of these six testified that they were in favor of the use of opium in China. Of the twenty-six merchants in the group, nineteen were favorable to opium, four were unfavorable, and three were doubtful. Foster further noted that only one of the twenty-six could be said to have extensive knowledge of the Chinese language and customs.[80]

Foster dismissed the conclusion of the Commission that opium use in China was comparable to the use of alcohol in Britain by saying that this was a fallacy commonly held by the pro-opium party in Britain. To refute the statement, he mentioned that opium was frequently used as a means of committing suicide but that alcohol was not. All the doctors testifying before the Commission, except one who was also in favor of opium use, said that opium was commonly used to commit suicide in China.[81]

In his appeal to overturn the conclusions of the Commission and end the opium trade, Foster wrote that he thought it was impossible for China to ever rise from its present weak condition unless it could first rid itself of the opium evil. He said that the nation that helped China end the opium evil would be China's greatest benefactor. He also stated his fear that other European nations might try to enter the opium trade, since a British royal commission had investigated the moral question of the trade and determined that it was not immoral and that the evils arising from the use of opium were slight. He said that the hypocrisy of the British concerning the opium trade had long been a byword among the other nations of the world.[82]

As Foster's work all too vividly pointed out, the Royal Commission on Opium was not an impartial body seeking to learn the truth about the opium question. The Commission's report defended the status quo and left the anti-opium advocates with their unfinished task of stopping the opium trade. Indeed, the Commission, which they had opposed from the first, hindered their efforts, because once the government had duly investigated the problem, it felt no need to discuss the matter further. The anti-opium forces were left to carry on their efforts outside Parliament in the hope that by convincing the British public that opium was harmful the immoral involvement of the British government would cease.

THE UNITED STATES PHILIPPINE COMMISSION ON OPIUM

Ten years after the British Royal Commission on Opium did its work, the United States government in the Philippines decided to investigate the problem of the use of opium, but the Philippine Commission was much less controversial than the British one had been and proved to have a greater impact on the ending of the opium trade from India to China, despite the fact that the trade was not its concern. The Philippine Commission had only three members— José Albert, M.D., a Filipino; the Right Rev. Charles H. Brent, Episcopal bishop of the Philippine Islands; and Edward C. Carter, a major in the United States Army—and a single secretary. (In 1903, the Canadian-born Bishop Brent had urged a detailed study of opium be undertaken, and when the Commission was organized he was appointed to it. He later served as president of the International Opium Commission which met in Shanghai, and the International Opium Conference at The Hague.[83]) The Philippine Commission was appointed to investigate the opium problem not to appease anti-opium forces at home or to support a position of the government that created it. Thus its work was less biased and its conclusions more apt to be supported by those who wished more information on the subject of opium and the opium trade. Although the United States government had no direct interest in the opium trade, it was concerned about the use of the drug, particularly among Chinese living in the Philippines, which the United States had recently acquired.

The Philippine Commission was charged with studying laws regulating the use and trade of opium in Japan, Tai-

wan, Burma, Java, and other countries the civil governor
designated. The Commission's members visited Japan, Taiwan, Hong Kong, Saigon, Singapore, Burma, and Java as
well as places in the Philippines. William Howard Taft, civil
governor of the Philippines, gave the Commission the wid-
est latitude to make whatever investigation it deemed necessary to carry out its work.[84] This freedom and the small
size of the Commission made it possible for its members to
function effectively.

On its visit to Shanghai the Commission met with American diplomats, British and American missionaries, and
Chinese and Western businessmen.[85] The testimony of the
diplomats and missionaries was that opium use was harmful and that moderate use of the drug was almost unknown.
Dr. W.H. Boone told the Commission that the use of opium
among women and children was increasing and that yearly
more and more opium was being harvested in China. He
thought the Chinese were growing more opium because it
offered a quick, large, profit, although he noted that pro-
opium Britishers said the Chinese were increasing their
production with the aim of taking over the British share of
the trade by exporting opium to other countries. Dr. Boone
told the Commission that he and other medical missionaries had submitted similar evidence to the Royal Commission on Opium, although the members of the Philippine
Commission could find no such evidence in the proceedings of the Royal Commission. Other missionaries also gave
testimony to the Philippine Commission, including several
who had long been active in the Anti-Opium League. A
group of Chinese merchants from Shanghai also gave evidence. Several of them stated that only the poor in China
smoked opium, but all agreed that opium smoking was
harmful and they wished that its use in China might be
ended.[86]

The Philippine Commission also sought information
from Western business firms in China. The examining phy-

sician of the Shanghai office of the New York Life Insur-
ance Company, Dr. N. Macleod, was questioned. He stated
that he believed some Chinese could use opium moderately
for years without suffering ill effects, but he also acknowledged that many were injured by it. He said his company
did not refuse to hire opium users, but it did try to determine the general health of the user and the amount of the
drug consumed daily.[87]

In Hong Kong, a Chinese merchant employed by the
China-American Commercial Company told the Commission that a nonuser was always preferred as an employee if
there were a choice between an opium smoker and a nonuser. He estimated that about one-third of the population
of Hong Kong used opium and said that the effects of its
use were all bad. A Chinese employee of Jardine, Matheson
and Company confirmed that nonsmokers were preferred
as employees.[88]

The evidence the Commission gathered in other cities
generally supported the opinions expressed in China that
opium was harmful and that there were few, if any, moderate users. The Commission reported its findings: opium
use had increased recently in the Philippines despite a high
tariff, smuggling of opium was common, and any attempt
by the government to raise revenue from opium would expose it to criticism. The Commission also opposed allowing local officials to try to control opium. It also reported
that any attempt to devise a system of opium farms would
only lead to more smuggling and the charge that the government sought revenue from a vice. Immediate prohibition of opium was thought unwise as it would create a
hardship on those already addicted to the drug. The Commission thought the best solution to the opium problem in
the Philippines was to create a monopoly and to make sure
that the revenues from the monopoly did not exceed the
expenses it incurred. Accordingly, the Commission recommended that opium immediately be made a strict govern-

ment monopoly and that all importation of the drug cease
after three years, except for that purchased by the government monopoly or used for medical purposes.[89]

Licenses were to be issued to Philippine residents who
were then addicts, and the drug was forbidden to others.
Addicts were prohibited from voting or holding public office. The Commission also recommended that children be
taught in the schools that opium was an evil and debasing
habit. The cultivation of opium in the Philippines was to
be strictly forbidden and opium dens outlawed. Anyone
seeking medical help to cure the opium habit would be
treated free of charge in the government hospitals if he were
indigent.[90]

While the actions of the Philippine Commission sought
to restrict the use of opium in the Philippines, the Commission had a greater impact in arousing opinion against
opium, particularly in China. In attempting to determine
why among all the peoples of the world the Chinese were
the most addicted to opium, the Commission wrote a stunning indictment of Chinese society. The report of the Commission was translated and widely circulated in China and
did much to arouse the Chinese against the drug.

The Commission's report stated, "The Chinese on the
whole are a moral, law-abiding, industrious and frugal
people. How comes it then that they are addicted, more
perhaps than any other race, to opium smoking and gambling, whose effects lead certainly to wastefulness and lazi-
ness, and generally to law-breaking and immorality?" The
report noted that if this question could be answered "we
shall have solved one problem connected with the use of
opium in China." It also noted that, despite "well-worded
edicts, letters, petitions, and literature condemnatory of
opium," the government of China took no action to "prohibit or limit its use" and that Chinese government officials understood their people "better than foreigners do or
can; and it is not conceivable that all or even a majority of

the ruling class in China willfully and deliberately encourages a custom which they all agree in condemning. And yet we find the opium vice, fulminated against by priest and illuminate, condemned and vilified by merchant and laborer, steadily increasing and spreading more and more widely."[91]

The report suggested that perhaps such questions were incomprehensible or imponderable for any non-Chinese, but if such answers could be found it would perhaps help them in making decisions regarding opium in the Philippines. The report continued with its most stunning indictment of China: "There seems to be in China neither a public opinion which controls nor a national life which welds and consolidates a people. There is no Chinese nation, there is merely a Chinese race." The report criticized the Chinese concern for family instead of nation, describing it as a "selfishness which acts as a positive force in urging men to sell opium to others of a different family or clan for it is no matter how many persons are debauched provided only those of the debaucher's family are not harmed but benefited." It also condemned the Chinese concept of duty "first and only to his family, that not only is he not his brother's keeper, but it is also his highest and paramount duty to benefit his family, even though it be by destroying morally and physically others not connected with his family. To him the injury of the many for the benefit of the few may be a righteous duty, provided the few are his family and the many are not." The report continued that "this peculiar altruistic selfishness" was also the root of Chinese "frugality, patience, laboriousness and well-recognized commercial honesty; and it may not be denied that this characteristic is often, if not generally, a great power for good. It is well known that there are many able, conscientious Chinese rulers, and many Chinese whom broad charity and uprightness make worthy of profound respect and admiration."[92]

Yet the report continued that the Chinese had few forms of entertainment and amusement. It said, "Absolute dullness and dreariness seem to prevail everywhere. . . . As an individual may by habitual toil and attention to business become incapable of amusement, so a race of almost incredible antiquity, which has toiled for millenniums, may likewise reach a point in its development where the faculty of being amused may have atrophied and disappeared, so that all that remains of that desire is to spend leisure in placidity. And nothing contributes to this so much as opium." The report also stated that "if the Chinese seem more easily to contract habits than other nations, and [be] more the slaves of them, is not that due to the dullness of the lives of the well-to-do and to the painful squalor of the indigent?" The Commissioners were willing to give the Chinese the benefit of the doubt that they were sincere in denouncing the use of opium, but it noted that little was done to try to limit the importation and use of opium. They wrote, "The Chinese government, at Shanghai, at any rate, does nothing more than place a somewhat heavy duty and tax on opium. So far as the Committee was able to determine, no special measure to discourage or limit the use of opium exists in Shanghai."[93]

The Commission noted that its work produced "no evidence" that the Chinese government was making "any earnest effort to diminish the use of opium." It pointed out that "certain . . . high officials wrote the most eloquent letters, condemnatory of the opium traffic, and appealing to foreign nations to prevent its introduction into China," yet these individuals were believed to "have steadily increased the areas under opium cultivation in their own domains." The Commission concluded that it was the intention of the Chinese to exclude the British from the opium trade so that they might monopolize it themselves.[94]

The Commission noted that it would be very hard to suppress the use of opium in China without the cooperation

of the central government. One Chinese witness had testified that a governor had attempted to suppress opium in
his province but was shortly replaced by the central government. The opium suppression was not carried on by his
successor.[95]

This assessment of Chinese society and the reasons Chinese used opium in far greater numbers than other peoples
was apparently not intended as a blanket indictment of the
Chinese people, because the report did include mention of
the positive aspects of Chinese life. However, the report was
issued in 1905 and a Chinese translation, done shortly there-
after, was widely circulated in China and quickly became
another bit of fuel to feed the fires of growing Chinese nationalism, particularly among returned students. Thus, what
was begun as an investigation to determine what the policy
of the United States government in the Philippines should
be toward the use of opium there resulted in the publication of an important piece of literature in the anti-opium
campaign in China.

If the pro-opium advocates had had their way, the Indian
opium trade would have continued forever. The demand
was unceasing; the profits were good, and many made fortunes dealing in the drug. But arrayed against the pro-
opium people were forces over which they had no control—
the growing medical evidence of the dangers of opium, the
Chinese awakening to the harm the drug wrought on their
people, and the increasing recognition in Britain and elsewhere of the immoral aspect of the opium trade. The missionaries would have added that God was also against anyone who supported the opium trade. But, most significant,
time was against the pro-opium faction. Time was limited
for the opium trade in the last years of the nineteenth century, as the anti-opium cause was gaining the momentum
that would doom the trade shortly after the turn of the new
century.

— FOUR —
The Anti-Opium Lobby
Comes of Age

In the last decade of the Ch'ing dynasty, reforms of the government, the military, and education were implemented in response to the growing public demands for change from the traditional ways. The most successful of these reforms was opium suppression.[1] Medical evidence of the dangers of using the drug had been accumulating for years and now public opinion demanded an end to the curse that had plagued China for centuries. Students returning from abroad joined the call for reform, because they realized that while many countries had drug problems, none had a problem as serious as China's. More important, the people of the Western nations and Japan viewed the Chinese with contempt because of the opium problem. Many of these students were involved in the various organizations that were seeking reform and/or the overthrow of the dynasty. However, they realized that whatever government the country had, China could not be a strong nation capable of dealing with other nations on a basis of equality if the country could not rid itself of the opium evil. In this milieu, the Ch'ing court issued an imperial edict prohibiting the use of the drug and negotiated an agreement with the British to end the opium trade from India. There was also a revival of the anti-opium societies during this period. These efforts at controlling opium also resulted in the first of the international drug conferences, which met at Shanghai in 1909 and at The Hague in 1913, for the purposes of establishing international cooperation to control opium and other dangerous drugs.

THE 1906 ANTI-OPIUM EDICT

On 20 September 1906, in response to the rising tide of opinion in China that now opposed the use of opium and recognized the harm it did to the Chinese people, an imperial edict was issued prohibiting the use of the drug. This edict differed from those issued earlier because it called for the suppression of domestic cultivation of opium poppies, which had recently become a serious problem. The edict was accompanied by specific regulations to eradicate opium use. The edict read,

> Since the restrictions against the use of opium were removed the poison of this drug has practically permeated the whole of China. The opium smoker wastes time and neglects work, ruins his health, and impoverishes his family, and the poverty and weakness which for the past few decades have been daily increasing amongst us are undoubtedly attributable to this cause. To speak of this arouses Our indignation, and, at a moment when We are striving to strengthen the Empire, it behooves Us to admonish the people, that all may realize the necessity of freeing themselves from these coils, and thus pass from sickness into health.
>
> It is hereby commanded that within a period of ten years the evils arising from foreign and native opium be equally and completely eradicated. Let the Government Council frame such measures as may be suitable and necessary for strictly forbidding the consumption of the drug and the cultivation of the poppy, and let them submit their proposals for Our approval.[2]

Along with the edict, the government issued ten "regulations prohibiting opium smoking." Regulation One stated that "to limit the cultivation of the poppy is the way to eradicate the evil." It went on to note that the poppy was widely cultivated, particularly in the provinces of Szechwan, Shensi, Kansu, Yunnan, Kweichow, and Shansi. Viceroys and governors were to instruct magistrates that they had to register all land then under poppy cultivation. No land not then in poppies was to be used for growing them, and land in poppies was to be reduced by one-tenth each year until all cultivation was eliminated. The regulation said, "Any person violating this rule will forfeit his land, and any person ceasing to grow the poppy and adopting some other crop before the time required by the Decree shall be considered as meriting special reward."[3]

Regulation Two stipulated that certificates be issued to all opium smokers to "prevent the possibility of new smokers." The government estimated that three-tenths or four-tenths of the people smoked opium and noted, "We must be lenient to those who have already acquired the habit, but must be strict for the future." The gentry and officials were called on to set the example for the common people. Under this regulation everyone, whatever his status, was to report his addiction to the local yamen, which would issue him a permit to purchase opium. Anyone caught buying opium secretly and without a permit was to be punished.

Regulation Three called for the gradual reduction of the amount of opium the addicts smoked. Anyone over the age of sixty was to be treated leniently, because of age, but younger addicts were to be issued a second certificate calling for a yearly reduction of their consumption by two-tenths or three-tenths and setting the date when they would cease smoking the drug. When a person ceased to smoke opium and his neighbors could testify to the fact at the yamen, his name was to be removed from the register and his certificate returned to the yamen. All addicts under the age of sixty who did not give up the opium habit were to be reported to a higher yamen and their names were to be made public so that they would not be treated "as equals of the general public."

Opium shops were ordered closed by Regulation Four, but it was noted this could not be done until the date for the complete prohibition of the drug was determined. However, those shops that enticed the young to try the drug were to be closed within six months. Restaurants and bars were not allowed to keep opium for their customers, who were also prohibited from bringing in pipes in order to smoke opium in these places. The regulations said, "If there are any who violate the rule, they shall be severely punished." Taxes on opium lamps were not to be collected after three months, and the sale of opium lamps, pipes, and other utensils was to be prohibited after six months.

Every opium shop was ordered to register, so that the exact number of them would be known, under the provisions of Regulation Five. Certificates were to be issued to the owners and they would be required to show these when purchasing the drug. No new opium shops were to be permitted. The amount of opium and opium dross these shops sold was to be reported to the local yamen so the officials could determine the amount to be reduced each year to effect total prohibition. Any surplus at the time of total prohibition was to be confiscated and a fine, double the value of the opium, levied.

Regulation Six asked that medical students in each province work on determining the best cure for the opium habit. The pills they manufactured were to be inexpensive and not to contain opium or morphia and were to be distributed throughout each province and sold at cost. Poor people were to receive the pills free.

Anti-opium societies to aid the addicts in breaking their habits were ordered established by Regulation Seven. However, these societies were to focus on anti-opium issues and were cautioned not to "discuss any other matters, such as political questions bearing on topical affairs or local administration, or any other matters."

Regulation Eight stressed that local officials and local

gentry would be heavily relied upon for the suppression of poppy cultivation and opium smoking. They were to report statistics on the area under cultivation, the number of smokers, the amount of anti-opium pills sold, and the number of anti-opium societies in their areas. Irregularities were not to be permitted and any official found guilty of an irregularity or bribery was to be punished for fraud.

Officials who were opium smokers were the subject of Regulation Nine, which directed them to set the example for the common people and required them to give up the habit more rapidly. Officials over the age of sixty were exempted from the regulations because of their age, but all other officials, including princes, generals, and governors, were "not allowed to conceal their affairs, and if they smoke opium, they shall report themselves and the dates when they should stop" smoking. They were not allowed to retire from public affairs while curing themselves from the habit, and they were prohibited from taking opium for any illness as that would prolong the cure. Lower officials, such as metropolitan and provincial, civil and military officials, professors and students, were required to stop smoking within six months.

Regulation Ten noted that foreign opium was imported to China and instructed the *Wai-wu Pu* (Foreign Office) to undertake negotiations with the foreign powers to restrict the importation of opium gradually over a period of years so that importation would cease before the date of final prohibition in China. In cases where opium was being imported from countries with which China had no treaties, the importation was to be stopped under Chinese law. The commissioner of Customs was instructed to find a way to stop the importation of both opium and morphia at the frontiers.[4]

Further instructions were issued on 7 February 1907, calling for anti-opium societies to be extended and opium dens throughout the provinces to be closed according to the regulations. All Tartar generals, viceroys, and governors and their subordinates were to take a "conscientious" part in carrying out these provisions. More important, the instructions noted that cultivation of the poppy was to be strictly forbidden, so that within ten years it would be entirely abolished. Yet another set of instructions was issued on 26 June 1907, noting that the officials were to take strict measures to rid the country of the opium evil. "If an official merely keeps up appearances and, while outwardly obeying, secretly disregards these commands, he is to be denounced by name for punishment," the instructions read. Officials were to report annually to the central government the amount of opium land under other cultivation in their areas.[5]

Following the issuance of the edict and the regulations, numerous memorials were issued by government departments giving instructions as to how the prohibitions would be carried out. They also dealt with such matters as allowing properly licensed persons to purchase opium in various cities if they were traveling, surveillance throughout the countryside to assure that the prohibitions were being obeyed, and awards to those who promoted opium suppression.

Some officials who thought the gradual suppression of opium was not the ideal way to end the use of the drug sent memorials to the Throne. Among them was Hsi-liang, viceroy of Yunnan and Kweichow, who thought it would be possible to suppress the cultivation of opium in Yunnan on a much faster schedule but allowed that the accomplishment of this rested with the officials of that province. Another memorial, from Ch'en Chih-tai, the governor of Kiangsu, called for special penal laws for those selling morphia. He noted that morphia addiction was increasing since many people used it as a cure for the opium habit. He urged a strict prohibition against the manufacture and sale of morphia and instruments for its injection.[6] Other memorials stated that officials were complying with the provisions

of the imperial edict. These generally followed the style of
the Ningpo magistrates, prefects, and policemen, who had
issued memorials to the various districts of the province,
covering such topics as opium prohibition, the prohibition
of poppy cultivation, exhortations to farmers to raise cotton and grain instead of poppies, the closing of opium dens
and a prohibition that private houses could not be used as
opium dens, the registration of smokers and dens, and the
destruction of opium-smoking equipment.[7]

THE TEN-YEAR AGREEMENT WITH BRITAIN

Along with the domestic suppression of opium, the Chinese sought to restrict the importation of the drug, most of
which came from British India. The Chinese probably could
have refused to buy Indian opium, thus forcing an end to
the trade, but the Chinese opium suppression movement
coincided with a change in the political attitude in Britain,
which now favored an end to the involvement of the British
government in this trade.

The tide had finally turned in favor of the anti-opium
movement with the Parliamentary elections, which brought
the Liberals to office in 1906. The new Parliament was
mostly middle class and many of the new M.P.s were members of the nonconformist churches, which had long been
active in the crusade against opium. The elections also
brought to office nearly 250 candidates who had formally
expressed their support for the anti-opium cause. Under
the new government, John Morley became the head of the
India Office and Sir Edward Grey became foreign secretary. They were destined to play a large role in ending the
official opium traffic from India to China. Both had supported the 1891 Parliamentary motion of Sir Joseph Pease,
which had declared the opium traffic "morally indefensible."[8]

On 30 May 1906, a motion was made in Parliament "that

this House re-affirms its conviction that the Indo-Chinese Opium Trade is morally indefensible, and requests His Majesty's Government to take such steps as may be necessary for bringing it to a speedy close." Morley said that the cabinet had given him carte blanche to deal with the question of opium and he knew that opinion in England and Scotland was strongly against the trade. He said that the opium revenue then accounted for only 7 percent of the revenue of British India, although it was more important to the Native States. When the measure came up in Commons, he declared on behalf of the government that if China wanted to restrict the consumption of opium, "the British Government would not close the door . . . to any plan . . . brought forth in good faith . . . [and] would agree [to it] even though it might cost us some sacrifice."[9] The motion was approved without division, but Morley wrote that, had a division occurred, the motion would have been carried by a two hundred vote majority.[10] Once the vote was taken, the anti-opium forces, a "'happy band of pilgrims' . . . who had fought so long to reach the goal now in sight, linked each other's arms and marched down from the lobby to the street singing the doxology."[11]

It should be noted that the Chinese official, T'ang Shao-yi, on a trip to India in 1905, had been told by Finance Minister Edward Baker that the Indian government could do without the revenue it gained from opium. The statement was repeated in some correspondence of the India Office but little, if anything, was ever said about it in Parliament. The remark can be attributed either to Baker's reputation for being impulsive or to his desire to rid the government of the inconvenience of the great fluctuations in the funds it gained from the opium revenues.[12]

Following their 1906 edict suppressing opium, the Chinese formally requested that the British end the opium trade from India.[13] The Chinese sent their request to the British on 26 January 1907, but it was 12 August before the British

responded. The delay was the result of the need for correspondence between India and London on the matter. Finally, the British agreed that the annual export of opium
would be reduced by one-tenth annually for ten years provided the Chinese made corresponding reductions in the
domestic production of opium. The agreement was to last
for an experimental period of three years, but it would be
extended to run the entire ten years if the Chinese kept
their part of the agreement by suppressing the drug in
China. The agreement went into effect on 1 January 1908,
at the insistence of the Chinese. The British had hoped to
delay implementing it until July of that year, but the Chinese insisted that was unrealistic, since the poppy would be
gone from many parts of China by that date. The agreement called for the Indian government to reduce the gross
export of opium based on the average amount imported
into China in the years 1901 to 1905. The amount of 51,000
chests was accepted as the base, with a reduction of 5,100
chests per year to begin in 1908. The British also agreed to
allow a Chinese government official to reside in Calcutta
for the purpose of inspecting the export of opium to China,
as long as he did not interfere with the trade. However, the
British opposed the Chinese proposal to double the tax on
Indian opium on the grounds that it was twice as strong as
the native drug. The British argued that the Chinese drug
had improved in recent years and that there was no scientific basis to prove the strength of one variety compared to
another. However, the British did agree to restrict the export of opium to Hong Kong and to curtail smuggling from
Hong Kong to China. It should be noted that the three-
year trial period was insisted upon by the British government because very few Britishers thought the Chinese were
sincere in their desire to rid themselves of the opium problem. Many Englishmen thought the Chinese were seeking
to suppress the Indian drug so that they might monopolize

the trade for themselves. Sir Edward Grey suggested that Sir Alexander Hosie undertake an investigation of poppy cultivation in western China to see if the Chinese were keeping their part of the agreement and suppressing domestic poppy cultivation. Chinese officials agreed to the proposal.[14]

THE ANTI-OPIUM SOCIETIES

As it became increasingly evident that there was growing popular support in China for opium suppression and particularly after the issuance of the 1906 edict, the missionary anti-opium societies renewed their efforts to end the use of the drug in China. Chinese anti-opium societies also sprang up in many areas, particularly as public opinion opposing opium use increased.

The Anti-Opium League, which had been active prior to the Boxer Uprising, renewed its efforts to convince addicts to give up the drug. Although the league's members were greatly encouraged by the 1906 edict, they recognized that they needed to continue their efforts if complete suppression of opium were to become a reality. For each provincial capital the league appointed an Executive Committee to "watch over the closing of the dens, the diminution of the poppy-acreage, and the sales of raw opium, and report the failures" to appropriate officials.[15]

In a letter to missionaries, the Rev. Hampden C. DuBose urged them not to relax their efforts against opium. He said that the next months would be crucial and noted that he had a report from Hsuchow, Kiangsu, which said, "The poppy this year was pulled up through fright; the few who kept the plant in their fields paid only a nominal tax; there is great danger lest the whole country grows the poppy next year." As with all such letters DuBose asked for money for the Anti-Opium League. Missionaries were urged not to forget the churches at home. DuBose called for them to

"Hear the voice from Heaven, 'Write.' Write to papers at home, religious and secular, city and village on opium reform in China."[16]

The Chinese delegation to the International Opium Commission in Shanghai in 1909 reported on the work of the anti-opium societies in Fukien, stating they had issued fifty-six letters and documents "urging the people to give up the opium habit and striving to create a sentiment against opium." Both the Anti-Opium League and the Chinese anti-opium societies were active in public burnings of opium equipment. The Fukien anti-opium society held eight public burnings of opium and opium-smoking equipment with the following destruction reported: 4,433 pipes, 4,482 pipe bowls, 3,693 lamps, 3,497 boxes, 3,620 plates, 8,971 needles, 427 large and 87 small cooking vessels, plus 3,138 ounces of opium and 577 ounces of opium deposits from pipes.[17]

After the issuance of the 1906 edict the Chinese government appointed seven mandarins with plenipotentiary powers to act as the Governmental Opium Commission. They were to "travel from province to province and prefecture to prefecture, closing the dens, destroying the fields of poppy, cashiering the opium-smoking officials, shutting up the raw opium hongs, strengthening the hands of the Anti-Opium Societies, helping the poor inebriates to get rid of the craving and with the iron rod of Anti-opium breaking in pieces the potters' vessels of poison."[18]

As these anti-opium activities increased, some Chinese officials came to realize that the missionaries, with whom they had many differences on other issues, could be useful allies in the fight against opium. Nanking Viceroy Tuan Fang wrote to the Reverend DuBose in 1908, saying, "Your whole-hearted exhortations in the anti-opium cause, [and] the fame of your benevolence commands the respect of all both far and near."[19] And the Throne took note of the work of the foreigners in combating opium in an imperial decree dated 22 March 1908. The decree outlined the evils of opium and the harm it brought to China and mentioned the fact that officials, gentry, literati, and common people were now urging that the drug be given up. The decree acknowledged that people from various countries were active in the movement and that many had made anti-opium medicines. The foreigners "show deep regret in seeing that the people of China do not abolish the drug from the country. If people of other countries show this feeling, how much more should it be our duty who have this fatal habit among us to use our best endeavors to eradicate the habit from our midst."[20] The decree continued mentioning the 1906 anti-opium edict and the 1907 agreement with Britain calling for the ten-year reduction of the opium trade. It cautioned, "Once we fail, it is to be feared that the opportunity may not come again to us. If we should ourselves eternally be unable to get rid of the fatal habit we shall be a lost country. When one thinks of this, from the Emperor on his Throne, the Ministers with him, down to the meanest subject, all ought to be filled with shame, alarm and uneasiness."[21]

In attempting to learn how widespread was the popular support against opium, the Anti-Opium League in 1908 sent out questionnaires to mission stations throughout China asking the status of anti-opium movements in each area. The 180 responses indicated that, except in some small areas where there was indifference, there was general enthusiasm for opium reform. The respondents reported that support come from the upper classes, who recognized that opium suppression was for the public good, and from the merchants and farmers, who saw it as a means of national reform. Those who opposed the reform either could not see the benefits of refraining from opium use or thought officials would be unable to cope with the task of suppression. From Szechwan came the report, "As this is an opium center the people fear the spoiling of their business and therefore public opinion is against the suppression of the trade."[22]

Members of the Anti-Opium League saw public opinion finally coming to support the position they had maintained for years. They said that the bell was finally tolling for the opium trade and that the work of so many in the past was finally bearing fruit. The long-ago petition of the clergymen of the Church of England and the speeches in the House of Commons on the moral issue involved in the official opium trade were finally resulting in the removal of the curse from the Chinese countryside. Five years from the opening of the International Opium Commission meetings in Shanghai (31 December 1914) the Anti-Opium League predicted, "The funeral rites of poppy and opium will be performed, and glad hosannah resound, from desert to sea."[23]

With the success of the anti-opium crusade in China, the missionaries could point to at least one area where their years of effort had paid off. One Westerner in conversation with the Reverend DuBose said the evangelistic efforts of the missionaries had borne little fruit. DuBose agreed if the man meant converts, but "if we look at opium there was more accomplished in the months of April, May, and [June] this year than in the three score and ten years that are past." The man agreed and said, "I see your meaning. The progress for a century has been slow; there may soon be large and rapid in-gatherings into the church."[24] Such must have been the wish of countless missionaries. Since none of the churches allowed opium addicts into membership, the missionaries now saw vast numbers of former addicts as potential converts. To the missionaries who had had their attention and efforts diverted from preaching the Gospel to fighting opium, surely the predicted end of the opium problem came as a welcome relief. The end had come, not only through the missionaries' efforts, but also as the result of the changed attitudes on the part of the Chinese, who now encouraged the domestic suppression of the opium evil, and on the part of the British, who now favored the end of the government's involvement in the opium trade. Nonetheless, the missionaries were pleased.

THE 1907 PROTESTANT MISSIONARY CONFERENCE

In 1907 the Protestant missionaries held the China Centenary Missionary Conference at Shanghai and discussed their anti-opium work and the successes of the recent reform movement in China. Because of the government's anti-opium decree, more and more people were seeking help in the opium refuges the missionaries ran. They viewed this as a new opportunity to make contacts with Chinese who might otherwise have never come into close contact with Christians.

In resolutions adopted by the conference, the missionaries reaffirmed their opposition to the opium trade, which they had stated at the Missionary Conference in 1877 and reaffirmed at the one in 1890. They expressed their thankfulness for the efforts of the British and Chinese governments to end the trade and the use of opium and morphia in China. The missionaries praised the Chinese government for its ten-year plan to suppress the use of the drug and noted that they believed the government was sincere in its efforts, regardless of the final success or failure of the campaign. They also stated that regardless of the outcome of the Chinese government's program, it was the missionaries' conviction that nothing could justify the continuation of any government or individual in the demoralization of the Chinese people with opium—not even the pretext that the rulers of China were doing the same.[25]

The conference also resolved "to urge Christians in all lands where numbers of Chinese are living to earnestly cooperate in securing public sentiment against the use and sale of opium."[26] In discussing this resolution, Arnold Fos-

ter expressed the opinion that the officials who were pres-
ently in charge of opium suppression were themselves
opium addicts. He also feared that if the opium revenue
abruptly ended and no new revenues were found to replace
them, there would be a negative reaction to the opium suppression campaign. Dr. William H. Park urged that the
church reaffirm its stand that church members could not
smoke opium, grow poppies on their land, sell the drug,
rent houses for use as opium dens, or engage in selling the
anti-opium remedies that contained opium and its derivatives. He also urged the missionaries to join with the Chinese in the anti-opium societies they were beginning to establish throughout the country. He noted that the Chinese
were capable of leading the anti-opium societies but that
many welcomed the help of the missionaries, who had long
been opposed to opium. Archdeacon Arthur E. Moule
noted that he had opposed opium at the 1877 Missionary
Conference and continued to do so. He reported that upon
his return from England five years earlier he had been hor-
rified to find that opium smoking was "no longer regarded
with shame, but was becoming fashionable." He said he was
astonished at the change in attitude toward opium that had
come over Britain and China in recent years but hoped that
it would bring an end to the opium curse.[27]

THE OPIUM REFUGES AND CURES FOR ADDICTION

The missionaries had long been concerned with trying to
cure opium addicts of their habits, but the problem became
more crucial with the decision of the government to prohibit the use of the drug. As early as the 1860s, both medical and nonmedical missionaries established opium refuges
where they sought to cure those who voluntarily came for
help. The primary aim of many of the missionaries was to
cure the addicts so that they might be admitted to church
membership. Within an opium refuge run by missionaries,

the addicts were treated to liberal doses of Christianity as they withdrew from their dependence on the drug. In 1906 the American Board of Commissioners for Foreign Missions reported that in one of their refuges "morning and evening prayers were held with the patients. They are taught Christian hymns, the Ten Commandments, the Lord's Prayer. The period of enforced seclusion and idleness gives great opportunity for sowing the seed, and good soil is often found in the hearts of men who are fighting victoriously with their greatest enemy."[28] Yet, as withdrawal symptoms became intense, Christianity alone was not enough to ease the suffering and the addicts would do almost anything to obtain opium to satisfy their cravings.

Missionaries reported a constant struggle to keep the refuge inmates from securing opium. The problems the missionaries had with their refuges were complicated by their lack of medical knowledge about the nature of opium addiction and the difficulties of withdrawal. Every missionary who ran a refuge reported the addicts suffered withdrawal symptoms, and this led to a debate on the best way to end addiction. Some missionaries favored complete withdrawal of the drug at the time the addict entered the refuge, while others favored gradual withdrawal over a period of weeks. Some of the missionaries tried pharmaceutical cures to ease the pains of withdrawal. In his survey of doctors, Dr. William H. Park had asked their opinions on the method they used to withdraw the drug from the addict. Of those replying, forty-one said they withdrew the drug suddenly, twenty-two said they withdrew it gradually, and seven said they used both methods, depending on the general condition of the patient. Of those who withdrew the drug suddenly, all reported the addicts suffered severe withdrawal symptoms. However, some doctors argued that these symptoms were the same as those the addicts suffered if the drug were withdrawn slowly.[29]

The problems of the refuges were vividly described by

the founder of one of the earliest refuges, the Rev. Frederich F. Gough of the Church Missionary Society in Ningpo. He started his work in the 1860s by taking addicts into his home to help them break the habit. Accepting several at a time, he treated a total of 133 patients, charging them each a small fee to cover his costs. He reported that after a few days without the pipe they "suffered agonies of craving . . . worse than any drunkard for drink." To obtain opium, Gough reported, the addicts lowered baskets through the windows to people outside who supplied them with the drug. When the windows were barred, the addicts broke down the bars. Inside the refuge, as the withdrawal symptoms became worse, "violent quarrels took place, tempers being irritated by restraint and by the sight of some securing the longed-for drug." Others reported that the best opium refuge had high walls, no windows, and a gatekeeper who was absolutely incorruptible. Although the opium addicts had voluntarily sought help in the refuge, many wanted to leave once the withdrawal symptoms began. Many missionaries required that addicts promise to stay in the refuge until cured of the habit, but only the strongest and most determined addicts were able to endure the cure, and only the strongest and most determined missionaries were able to endure the groans and pleading of the addicts.[30]

The Rev. Moir Duncan of the English Baptist Mission in Shensi wrote of the opium refuge he ran that "voluntary endurance of a few days' misery was evidence that the men were sincere in their wish to abjure the evil habit." Yet he noted that he sometimes had to use force to get the patients to stay, as "some scaled the walls during the night, [and] some groaned to elicit pity and relax stringency." He said it was impossible to know how many remained free of the drug after leaving the refuge.[31]

The methods of curing the opium habit were much debated by medical doctors. Cures ran the gamut from the latest opium derivatives to home remedies. Some mission-

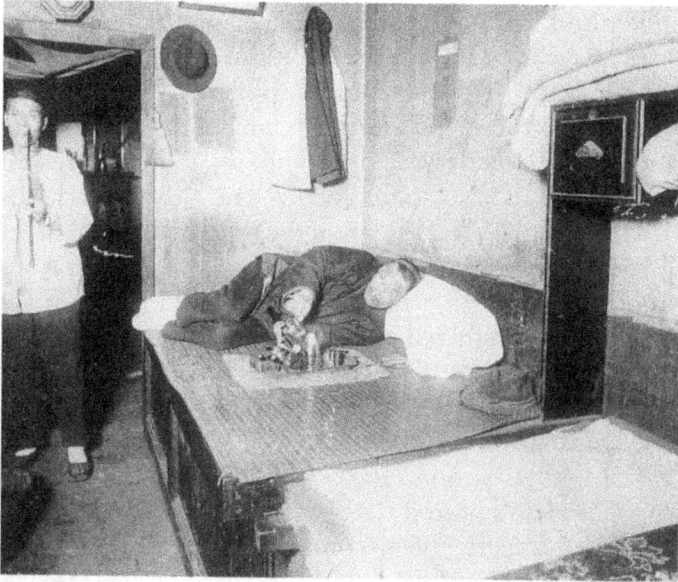

An underground opium den with mats for smokers to
recline on. The photo was taken with a flash. Library
of Congress.

aries who lacked funds to purchase opium cures reported
they had good success simply by withdrawing the drug and
feeding the addict good food. Within a few days, they reported, the addict was cured.[32] Because medical science had
not yet acquired adequate information on opium derivatives, many of them were thought to be the answer to the
opium addicts' problem. Anti-opium pills, usually containing morphine, were widespread in China in the late nineteenth and early twentieth centuries. Dr. John Dudgeon sold
anti-opium pills containing morphine in a street shop near
his hospital. Other doctors sold pills containing quinine or
belladonna or combinations of both.

In his survey of physicians, Park asked if opium addicts
desired to break the habit and if they could do it alone.
Nearly all the doctors replied that addicts did desire to stop

134 CRUSADERS AGAINST OPIUM

using opium, although some qualified their answers by saying addicts wished to stop the habit if it could be done painlessly. Dr. Henry M. McCandliss replied, "Yes, if someone
else could do the suffering for them." Most of the doctors
acknowledged that it was possible for an addict to break the
habit by himself, but some doctors said this was rare for a
confirmed addict. Yet, nearly all the doctors knew of at least
one such case. Almost all the doctors also said that anti-
opium pills containing morphine were sold freely in their
areas. Some recognized the dangers of the pills and suggested that they should be banned by the Chinese authorities. Indeed, the value of morphine entering China increased dramatically in the 1890s, when it entered duty free.
The Shanghai Customs House reported that 15,711 ounces
of morphia had entered that port in 1892, but by 1897 the
amount had reached 68,170 ounces. This morphia was valued at $18,790 (Mexican) in 1892 and at $172,578 (Mexican)
in 1897.

In addition to morphia pills, hypodermic injections were
becoming more common in the late 1890s. Dr. Park reported that "ghouls, with hypodermic syringes and morphia
solutions up their sleeves, frequent the tea shops, giving
injections at seven cash a piece. Their victims stand in a
row and pass before them . . . they never cleanse their syringes, and when their solutions give out they prepare a
fresh supply, using dirty water found in the tea shops and
mixing it in cups that have not been properly washed since
the days of Yao and Shun."[33] The treatment incapacitated
many coolies, and Dr. Park knew of one death caused by it.

Some doctors even tried the morphia cure on their patients. Dr. Henry D. Porter reported that with anti-opium
pills "the danger is that it simply continued the habit under a new though very mild form," although he said that
minute doses of morphia given by injection seemed to produce more promising results.[34]

The wide range of cures was evident at the International Opium Commission meetings in 1909, where one American exhibited seventy-six opium cures that he had found contained opium.[35] Earlier in 1893, the Rev. George L. Mason of the American Baptist Missionary Union in Chekiang reported that in native shops one could purchase "dozens of preparations, liquids, powders, pills, lozenges, put up in attractive shape and flamingly advertised as sure cures of the opium habit." Some of these were made by foreigners and some by Chinese druggists, and of the seven Mason had analyzed all contained opium as the chief ingredient.[36]

A systematic study of anti-opium pills done in conjunction with the International Conference on Opium held at The Hague in 1912 revealed that virtually all of the eighty-nine brands contained morphia. The pills had such names as "Resurrection pill," "Awakening China anti-opium pill," "Heaven-made cure," "Cure for old habit," "Instantaneous cure," "Universal Salvation," "Benefit of Heaven," "Glorifying Heaven anti-opium powder," "Race protecting pill," and "A fortnight cure."[37]

Medical science lacked a real cure for the opium habit, but many doctors were experimenting with drugs and combinations of drugs. Dr. G. King reported he had had some success with quinine, nux vomica, phosphorus, and belladonna (Nux vomica was the seed of *Strychnos nux-vomica Linne*, commonly known as Quaker or bachelor's buttons). Dr. King reported that quinine alone was the least effective cure he had tried. Nux vomica was quite effective, but it worked too slowly for the opium addict, who needed an immediate cure. Phosphorus was the best cure and it was most effective when used in combination with quinine, nux vomica, or some other nerve stimulant. Phosphorus and belladonna used in combination were also thought to be quite effective. Unfortunately, Dr. King noted, most of these cures were too expensive for purchase by missionaries, but he reported the Kirby firm of London was willing to supply a special preparation of phosphorus, quinine, and nux vomica for anti-opium work only at a special reduced price for missionaries. At this special price the cures would cost only about one penny a day.[38]

Dr. King's prescriptions for curing the opium habit were disputed by Dr. Dudgeon, who noted that quinine was very effective but that its price was too high for it to be widely used. He preferred a pill he made, composed of camphor, extract of gentian, cinnamon, ginger, capsicum, and a quarter grain of Smyrna opium. Capsicum or cayenne pepper was an ingredient of many opium cures.[39]

Anti-opium pills containing opium were so commonly prescribed by the missionaries that they were known as "Jesus opium," much to the horror of those dispensing them. The distribution of pills containing opium derivatives by medical missionaries was denounced by the China Medical Missionary Association, which urged that church members not be allowed to use them.[40] Laudanum, the most common form of opium used in the Western countries, was also used as an opium cure in China, even though most doctors knew it was an opium derivative. Dudgeon noted that laudanum mixed with peppermint and quassia was as effective an opium cure as were morphine injections.[41]

Considering the cures the missionary doctors tried, the addict was probably better off if he went to a refuge run by a nonmedical missionary. Many such missionaries, lacking medical knowledge about drugs and the money to purchase the cures, simply withdrew the drug and fed the addict nourishing food. Many, to their surprise, found this to be an effective cure. Indeed, because many addicts chose to buy opium instead of food and because opium upset the digestive system, many addicts simply had not had proper nourishment for a long time. Once the body received food instead of opium, many addicts soon broke their dependence on the drug.[42]

THE INTERNATIONAL OPIUM COMMISSION

The British and the Chinese realized that their attempts to
end the India to China opium trade and the illegal use of
opium in China could not be successful without a much
wider effort to stop the illegal use and trade of opium and
its derivatives. Following the work done by the Philippine
Commission, the Americans, too, realized that international
controls for drugs were needed. Under the leadership of
President Theodore Roosevelt, the Americans urged that
an international conference be called to deal with the question of opium in China and more generally with the worldwide drug situation.

Accordingly, the International Opium Commission, the
first ever organized, met at Shanghai on 1 February 1909.
Countries sending delegates included Austria-Hungary,
China, France, Germany, Great Britain, Italy, Japan, Neth-
erlands, Persia, Portugal, Russia, Siam, and the United
States. Noteworthy among the delegates were the Right Rev.
Charles H. Brent, D.D., bishop of the Philippines, who be-
came president of the conference; His Excellency Tuan
Fang, viceroy of Kiangsi and Kiangsu; and Sir Alexander
Hosie, British consul-general in China. The conference di-
vided itself into seven committees, with Sir Alexander Hosie
serving on the committee to consider the "Growth of the
Poppy and the Production of Opium." He was assisted by
Hamilton Wright, M.D., a member of the United States
delegation, and the Honorable Lew Yuk-lin, a member of
the Chinese delegation.[43]

The Commission began its work with a statement by Tuan
Fang on the status of opium in China. He noted that the
1906 decree had called for a ten-year plan to abolish opium
production and use in China. He said there had already
been an 80 percent reduction in the Kiangnan area of
Kiangsu and that officials from six provinces—Shansi,
Yunnan, Fukien, Anhwei, Honan, and Heilungkiang—had

informed the throne that all opium poppies would be gone from their areas by winter. He noted that the officials and the gentry in many provinces were taking the lead in anti-opium societies to help addicts break the habit. He predicted that the cultivation of the poppy would be stopped entirely within the next several years.[44] In the opening session of the meeting, Bishop Brent noted that the delegates were not envoys extraordinary nor ministers plenipotentiary and, hence, any conclusions or recommendations they made would not be binding upon their governments.[45]

Much of the work of the Commission dealt with a study of the laws and actions of the countries represented in regard to opium and other drugs. On 8 February, T'ang Kuo-an presented a report on China, covering such topics as cultivation, production and consumption of opium; morphia; anti-opium remedies; and anti-opium measures. He acknowledged that it was extremely difficult to obtain adequate statistical information because of the lack of proper government machinery to collect such data. He stated that "about 25 percent of the total quantity of opium produced in China escaped taxation, and that the Imperial Exchequer received not more than one-third of the revenue actually collected, the remaining two-thirds being retained by the different provinces for local administrative purposes." He estimated that "more than 600,000 piculs of opium were consumed annually within the Empire up to the year 1906." T'ang also said that enormous quantities of morphia were being "imported clandestinely" to China. He called for action to stop the spread of anti-opium remedies, most of which contained opium or its derivatives. He described the task "as stupendous, and declared that the Chinese people were grappling earnestly with a problem greater than any that had ever confronted a nation in the history of the world."[46]

Addressing the Commission on 12 February, Sir Alexander Hosie called on the Chinese to furnish more accurate information on opium cultivation. He noted that as part of the opium suppression decree the government had called upon local officials to obtain this information for the central government. He said he thought rough approximations of the acreage under cultivation detracted from the value of the Commission's work, particularly when those approximations concerned the inland provinces where the largest amount of opium was produced. Hosie also took issue with some of the figures in the Chinese report. He said that it was impossible to tell where imported opium was being consumed in China, because once it entered the port and the tax on it was collected it might be transported anywhere in the empire without again coming under the scrutiny of the Customs Service. He also noted the big differences in the amounts of opium production reported within China and said that these reports were misleading. He also took issue with the report that opium cultivation would be suppressed by the following winter, since in some parts of China, notably Manchuria, opium was a summer crop.[47]

Hosie gave the Commission his own estimates on the number of opium smokers in China. He estimated them to be 6.64 percent of the adult population, taking into consideration women, many of whom were opium smokers. For adult men, he estimated the rate was 13 percent. He acknowledged, however, that his figures were based on the 1906 Customs reports on the amount of opium in China and he knew that these figures might be erroneous. He concluded by saying that the actual figures on the production and consumption of opium in China were still unknown, as there was no reliable way of compiling statistical data on the subject. The members of the Chinese delegation indicated that they accepted Hosie's criticism in the light in which it was made, since they knew he was sincerely interested in ending the opium evil in China.[48]

The question of anti-opium remedies was also considered by the Commission. T'ang Kuo-an stated that China was having difficulty suppressing the sale of these items and noted that all of them entered the country through the treaty ports and that it would be impossible to suppress them without the cooperation of the treaty powers.[49]

At a session on 23 February, Charles D. Tenney, Chinese secretary to the American legation, Peking, addressed the Commission, saying it was fortunate "that the deliberations . . . have not been disturbed by the clashing of extreme or hysterical views on one side or the other of the opium question. . . . The world knows and admits that opium and morphia constitute a danger that threatens the welfare of China, and . . . other nations." He also acknowledged that it was beyond question that the use of opium and morphia "enfeebles the will, diminishes the efficiency, and injures the characters of the people." He pointed out that of the nations at the meeting only China was not free to safeguard its people from opium use and they had "suffered most severely from the spread of the opium habit." Although he noted the inaccuracies in the Chinese reports to the Commission and the difficulties the Chinese government had in controlling various provinces, he thought the Chinese government was thoroughly committed to the anti-opium movement, that public sentiment was in favor of it, and that real progress had been made since the issuing of the Imperial Edict of 1906. He called upon the other nations to help the Chinese in their effort, as he stated the Chinese were like other people and thus capable of "earnest endeavor and great sacrifice" when it was to their benefit.[50]

T'ang Kuo-an, speaking on behalf of the Chinese delegation, acknowledged that the opium problem was a "most acute moral and economic question" and stated that however much other countries might help China in the end it was the Chinese who had to work for their own salvation. He noted that many thought China incapable of taking action against opium but acknowledged the efforts of those who had worked on China's behalf, particularly Lord Shaftesbury, Lord Morley, Sir Joseph Pease, Joseph G. Alexander, Benjamin Broomhall, and J. Hudson Taylor. T'ang thought it was normal to assume that the Chinese would not be able to "grapple successfully with the evil in her own borders." Yet he noted "the curse was so widespread, the difficulty of breaking the opium habit [was] so great, the clandestine use of the drug [was] so easy, and the difficulties [were] so baffling and enormous, that it [was] not strange if anyone should have conceived success to be impossible. To these doubts, however, the national sentiment against opium has proven an effective answer." He said that opium was the first question that had aroused the whole of the Chinese people to action. Because there was now the commitment to take action he asked the help of other nations. He noted, "It is a well-known fact that such an intensity is difficult to maintain over an extended period. The public mind cannot be kept centered for a long period of years upon a single reform. When a people is ready to abolish an evil, it should be done as soon as possible. Delay increases difficulties immeasurably." T'ang ended his statement by calling for China to have a "new relationship of friendship and understanding with the rest of the world" and by appealing to the others to recognize the higher moral law that transcends all else, "which through Confucius, says, 'Do not unto others what thou wouldst not have others do unto you,' and which through Jesus Christ, says, 'Thou shalt love thy neighbor as thyself.'"[51]

The resolutions adopted by the Commission acknowledged the sincerity of the Chinese government in its attempts to suppress opium throughout the country. The participating countries were urged to work for the gradual suppression of the practice of opium smoking in their territories. The use of opium for any but medicinal purposes was declared a matter for prohibition and careful regulation. The Commission found that each participating government had strict laws to prevent the smuggling of opium and urged their enforcement. The Commission also noted that the unrestricted manufacture and use of morphine was harmful and urged the various countries to take the necessary measures to control the spread of the morphine habit. Regarding anti-opium remedies, the Commission noted that it did not have the facilities to investigate them scientifically but urged that the various governments do so. Since the question of opium in the foreign concessions and settlements in China was a problem now that China was suppressing the drug, the Commission recommended the closing of the opium dens, the prohibition of the sale of anti-opium remedies containing opium, and the enforcement of the various countries' pharmacy laws in these areas.[52]

THE HAGUE CONFERENCE

The International Opium Commission that met in 1909 could only make recommendations and had no authority to make binding agreements, and many people recognized that its value had been limited. As a result of this shortcoming, American president William Howard Taft proposed that another conference be called and that the delegates have plenipotentiary powers. Accordingly, the second conference met at The Hague from 1 December 1911 to 23 January 1912. The same nations that had attended the 1909 meeting were present at the 1911-12 meeting, with the exception of Austria-Hungary, who declined while noting that the proceedings would be watched with sympathy. Turkey was also invited to The Hague Conference but did not attend. Prior to the meeting the United States government had sent to all participating nations a list of topics to be considered, including uniform national laws regulating the production, manufacture, and distribution of opium and its derivatives; restrictions on the number of ports opium-producing countries might use to ship the drug; measures to prevent opium

being shipped to countries that wished to restrict or prohibit its importation; notification of the countries involved
of the amount of the drug in international transit; regulations for the mailing of opium; and restriction and control
of the cultivation of the poppy so that no other nation would
attempt to fill the void created by China's and India's drop
in production. Other matters to be considered were: the
application of various governments' pharmacy laws to
the consular districts, concessions, and settlements in China;
the re-examination of treaty obligations and international
agreements under which the opium traffic was then regulated; uniform penal laws for offenses against the laws of
the powers regarding the production and traffic in opium;
uniform identifying marks for packages of opium in international transit; permits for opium exporters; the recipro-
cal right of search of vessels suspected of carrying contraband opium; measures to prevent the illegal use of flags by
vessels carrying opium; and the advisability of an international Commission to be entrusted with carrying out the
agreements.[53]

The British indicated their objections to several of the
points but added they would like to have morphia problems
dealt with at the conference. They also wished the conference to refrain from considering matters that had been regulated by treaty between Britain and China, as well as matters dealing with the production of opium for domestic use
in India and other British dominions.[54]

The Hague Conference was criticized by many anti-opium
leaders because they thought it would lack authority as long
as the British were not willing to have the question of their
trade with China discussed. However, the conference did
result in the signing of an international convention in which
all the contracting powers agreed to take measures to prevent the export of raw opium. With regard to prepared
opium, the contracting powers were to take measures to
gradually suppress its manufacture, trade, and use within

their countries, and its export was prohibited. Medicinal opium, morphine, and cocaine were also regulated under the terms of the treaty.[55]

With regard to China, the contracting powers that had treaties with China were to work in conjunction with the Chinese government to prevent the smuggling of opium and other drugs into Chinese territory, the powers' Asian colonies, and leased territories in China. The Chinese government was to take measures to prevent the smuggling of these drugs from China into the foreign colonies and leased territories. In addition, the Chinese government was to promulgate pharmacy laws regulating the sale of these drugs in China. Both the treaty powers and the Chinese were to take measures to restrict and control the habit of smoking opium, and opium dens were to be closed. The use of the drug in all places of entertainment was to be forbidden. All the nations attending the meeting signed the convention, but several did so with reservations. France reserved the right to have a separate ratification or denunciation for its protectorates. Britain signed, stating the convention would apply to India, Ceylon, the Straits Settlement, Hong Kong, and Wei Hai Wei but reserved the right to denounce the treaty for any other possessions. Persia and Siam also signed with reservations, since they were not treaty powers in China.[56]

The Shanghai Commission of 1909 and The Hague Conference of 1911-12 set the stage for further international conferences to deal with the problems of the international traffic in drugs. Another International Opium Conference was held at The Hague in 1913, and subsequent conferences were held under the auspices of the League of Nations. The international cooperation on the control of drugs, which had begun in China in 1909, continued with the purpose of protecting the other nations of the world from the evils of the unregulated and indiscriminate drug use that had plagued China for so long.

CHINA'S ECONOMIC QUESTION

Addressing the International Opium Commission in 1909, T'ang Kuo-an told the delegates that many people wondered how China would deal with the loss of revenues gained from opium. His response was that the Chinese people were so determined to end the use of opium in their country they would gladly pay new taxes on other items if it meant the country were free of the drug.[57] He continued that the economic burden of opium had become "almost unbearable." He cited as a conservative estimate 584,800 piculs of opium produced domestically in 1906: he valued it at Tls. 220 million. Added to the 1905 value for imported opium, Tls. 30 million, this meant that the Chinese had expended Tls. 250 million on the drug. The land that had been producing opium was now planted in wheat and other crops, which he estimated would yield an annual return of Tls. 150 million. This sum added to the other cost meant the cultivation of opium cost China Tls. 400 million per year. The social cost of the loss of productivity among addicts was even more difficult to determine, but it was thought to be Tls. 1,250,000 per day, for an annual loss of Tls. 456,250,000.

T'ang went on to note that opium also caused China to suffer a great loss of foreign trade. He acknowledged that other factors, such as inadequate transportation, the likin, and the small number of ports, hindered foreign trade, but he said that the poverty and inefficiency of the Chinese people, both of which were related to the opium evil, were the biggest factors preventing further development of China's international trade. He noted that China's attitude toward foreign trade was much different from what it had been fifty years earlier when all China wanted from abroad was opium and silver. He noted that cotton goods, kerosene oil, flour, and matches were among the imported items all Chinese now wanted. He said that "there can be no doubt about it, the opium traffic is *economically*, as well as morally, indefensible." He said that some special interests would suffer from the abolition of the opium trade if they failed to look beyond their immediate interests, but "there can be no doubt of the facts: opium is an economic loss to the world too great to be further endured."[58]

The question of the loss of revenue was on the minds of many people. In China, some opium merchants requested that the government delay suppressing the drug until they could sell their present stocks to avoid any loss of money![59] In Hong Kong, the government decided to make up its lost opium revenue by taxing wine and spirits. There was some opposition to this plan, but the government argued that it was the "least injurious form of new taxation which could have been devised."[60]

With regard to foreign trade, T'ang Kuo-an's statement that the Chinese now desired other products from abroad was borne out by the increase in the importation of certain goods. Kerosene imports increased yearly after the turn of the century as more and more Chinese, even in remote parts of the interior, began to demand the oil.[61] Imports of woolen and cotton goods were also increasing, particularly those from Britain, which were of better quality than the Russian fabric that was being imported to Manchuria. The Chinese were also importing industrial equipment for railroads and mines, as well as coal, since they did not then produce enough to meet their demands. Foodstuffs, particularly sugar and wheat flour, also increased among imports at this time.[62]

As the opium suppression campaign in China continued, it became evident even to skeptics that the Chinese were indeed serious about their desire to rid themselves of the drug. The change in the Chinese attitude toward opium coincided with a change in attitudes in the Western countries, which now favored control of opium and other drugs by domestic laws and international regulations. The missionaries viewed these changes as the results of their long years of effort but, except for the scientific evidence gathered by the medical missionaries, the changes in Chinese attitudes probably had little to do with the preaching of the missionaries on the evils of opium. Rather it was recognition by the Chinese that opium was harming their people, and, hence, must be carefully controlled.

In terms of economics, it became evident that other products would replace opium in China's imports and that lands planted in poppy would produce other crops that could be taxed by the government. Before the real economic impact of opium suppression could be felt, however, the 1911 revolution began disrupting the suppression movement, which had begun with successes far greater than even its most dedicated advocates could have hoped.

— FIVE —
Success and Failures of Opium Suppression

As the opium suppression campaign progressed, there were more and more signs that the Chinese were indeed sincere in their desire to rid their country of all opium. Those who doubted the motives of the Chinese soon had to admit they were dedicated to the effort and committed to seeing complete suppression a reality. Though the Ch'ing dynasty was weak and tottering, this did not stop many officials at all levels of the bureaucracy from trying to improve the country by eradicating poppy cultivation and the use of opium. Because the Chinese attitude toward opium had changed from toleration, or at least inaction concerning it, to intolerance, determination to rout out the evil was widespread. As the Chinese became increasingly aware of the fact that opium weakened them as a people and hindered their development into a modern nation, the suppression campaign became more aggressive. Of course, there were those who for personal or economic reasons did not wish the drug to be eliminated. Addicts faced the difficult task of breaking the habit. Merchants whose business was to import the drug from India, farmers who grew opium as a cash crop, and shopkeepers who operated opium dens all opposed suppression because it meant they would lose their incomes. Weaknesses existed in the government and nation in the closing years of the Ch'ing dynasty, but the success of the opium suppression campaign awakened many Chinese to the idea

that weaknesses need not be permanent and that change
was possible.

China's strength in the past had been sapped by the addiction of so many of its people to opium but, as the new
century neared the close of its first decade, increasing numbers of Chinese came to believe that China in the future
need not be weak for the same reason. As the Chinese awakened to the new possibilities for greatness, many of them
came to believe that if enough of them desired and worked
for it, they really could rid the country of the drug curse.
Many Chinese also realized that if they began such a crusade and failed they could not blame the failure on anyone
but themselves. The 1907 agreement with Britain was linked
to the domestic suppression of poppy cultivation, and the
success of that lay totally in the hands of the Chinese. In
their determination, the Chinese were ready to take action
against anyone who sought to continue the opium trade or
the use of the drug. The legalistic, business-as-usual attitude of the British concerning opium frequently conflicted
with the Chinese goals, and when it did the Chinese responded vigorously. No longer would Chinese allow foreigners to dictate what the Chinese would buy and use. China
was now determined to chart its own course. Unfortunately,
the drive to eliminate opium lost some of its momentum
with the 1911 revolution, which brought unrest to the countryside and conflicting ideas about what was best for China.

Under the 1907 agreement with Britain, the export of
Indian opium to China was to decrease as Chinese production declined.[1] The evidence of domestic suppression was
extensive, but the reliability of the Chinese statistics and
methods of collecting information left much to be desired
by the British. Tuan Fang told the International Opium
Commission in 1909 that opium cultivation was consider-
ably reduced. According to his report the poppy was totally
suppressed in Fengtien, while other areas reported 25 to

80 percent of the crop suppressed, with total eradication expected in most areas by the end of 1909. But no one knew precisely how much opium was still being produced in China, and estimates varied widely. In figures given to the International Opium Commission in 1909, Hosea Ballou Morse estimated that the total production in China in 1905 was 22,737,735 kilos. However, the Chinese Board of Revenue set the estimate for 1906 at 8,956,006 kilos. And these figures differed greatly from the 1906 estimate, based on Customs reports, which set the amount at 35,364,435 kilos. Customs reports also estimated the 1908 production would be 22,208,599 kilos.[2]

According to figures presented to the Commission, the foreign importation of opium actually increased slightly in 1907 following the 1906 edict banning domestic cultivation and use of the drug. Total importation was listed at 54,177 piculs in 1906 and 54,584 piculs in 1907. However, importation declined in 1908 to 48,397 piculs. In publishing its report, the Commission cautioned that it "acknowledged that accurate statistics about opium are most difficult to obtain in China, and it must therefore be understood that the figures given are in many cases only approximate and the result of sifting the scraps of information received here and there and the putting of 'two and two together' in the minds of the framers of the estimates." Estimating production in the southwestern provinces, which produced the largest amounts of opium, was especially difficult since the amount consumed locally was unknown and "taxation [was] irregular and, for the greater part, evaded, and where public or official returns are practically unknown."[3]

SIR ALEXANDER HOSIE'S INVESTIGATIONS

It was precisely this difficulty in obtaining reliable statistics from China and particularly from the provinces where most of the poppies were grown that made the British reluctant

to reduce the trade from India without some proof that the
Chinese were keeping their part of the 1907 agreement.
Unwilling to accept the reports of the Chinese that poppy
cultivation was being suppressed, the British insisted upon
sending their own inspector to investigate the extent of
poppy cultivation in the remote provinces. Sir Alexander
Hosie, who had served in the British diplomatic service in
several parts of China and who had long been interested
in the opium problem, was selected to undertake a major
investigation for the British in 1910-11 to report the success,
or failure, of the opium suppression campaign.

Following his investigation, Hosie sent reports to the British diplomats in Peking and published his findings in a two-
volume account, *On the Trail of the Opium Poppy*. His plan
was to visit the six provinces that produced most of China's
opium: Shansi, Shensi, Kansu, Szechwan, Yunnan, and
Kweichow. Beginning his travels in the late spring of 1910,
Hosie went first to Shansi, Shensi, and Kansu, it being too
late in the season to visit the southwestern provinces where
the poppy was then being harvested.[4]

Hosie began his journey in the city of T'aiyuan, Shansi,
where he met with Chinese government officials, including Ting Pao-ch'uan, governor of the province. In 1909 the
governor had invited a representative of the British legation to visit the province and he had been unable to find a
single poppy plant during a journey of four hundred miles.
Both Governor Ting and J.F. Brenan, the British consul,
told Hosie that there were no poppies growing in the province. In 1910 there had been an attempt to replant them in
one district but "repressive measures were taken, resulting
in the death by shooting of over twenty persons, the wound-
ing of over thirty, and the uprooting by troops of the young
plants."[5]

The governor reported that in 1904 there had been 1
million mou of poppies in the province, but when he arrived in 1905 he immediately set out to reduce its cultiva-

tion. By 1908 the area was down to 330,000 or 340,000 mou and in 1909 and 1910 no land was planted in poppies. There had been fifty-six wholesale opium establishments in Shansi, but all were closed in 1910. There were ten official opium refuges in the province and over four hundred unofficial ones, and the governor estimated that 100,000 addicts had been cured, 50 to 60 percent of them completely. Despite these reports, Hosie noted that the central government apparently was not satisfied that Shansi was completely free of the drug because on 27 September 1910, they had issued an edict listing the province as one where secret investigators had found poppies growing.[6] Yet, Hosie reported, the provincial officials "seemed to be justly proud of the achievement of their province" and "hinted" that they felt there should be a further reduction of imported opium because of the success of Shansi. Hosie told the officials that "the menace to China was not Indian but native-grown opium." The officials "seemed surprised when I told them that at the Shanghai Opium Commission the Chinese delegates . . . admitted that the annual production of opium in China amounted to about eight times the quantity annually imported from India and in former years had even exceeded that amount."[7]

Traveling by pony, Hosie was careful to avoid the main roads in favor of the less-traveled routes where he might be more likely to see poppies. He entered Shensi and traveled for five days before he saw any poppies, but he acknowledged that it would take months to travel up each valley so he admitted his observations were not complete. In Shensi, as well as in the other provinces he was to visit, Hosie found that in some out-of-the-way hamlets offices of the opium prohibition board had never been staffed. In all the provinces he visited he saw random poppies growing on the side of the road but dismissed them as unharvested stray plants from former poppy fields that were now planted in other crops. In his travels, Hosie frequently consulted with local missionaries on the extent of poppy cultivation in the area. Near Sian, Shensi, missionaries told him the poppy had in recent years been replaced by cereal grains, because officials were determined to eradicate poppy cultivation. On occasion, when he saw a field of poppies and tried to discover who owned it, he found the local people most reluctant to discuss the matter. In Shensi, as in other provinces, he sometimes found evidence of poppies concealed within fields of peas, wheat, or other grains. He also reported numerous poppy fields had been partially uprooted. At one place along the Wei River a farmer told Hosie that the previous year the area had been ablaze with poppies, but this year the officials were more stringent in their demands that poppies not be grown. As a result, all the farmers had planted cotton or sesamum in its place.[8]

In Sian, Hosie met the governor of Shensi, En Shou, who told him stringent measures had been taken to reduce poppy cultivation, with the result that a 60 to 80 percent reduction had been achieved in the last year and that the poppy would be gone by the following year. The governor stated that poppies "might still be found growing in out-of-the-way places and corners of the province, [but] cultivation might be considered as practically stopped." He also told Hosie that the people resented the suppression, but Hosie thought that would not stop the governor from continuing the suppression campaign. Hosie believed the reduction was about half the governor's estimate and that "the assurance given that no poppy would be grown in Shensi in 1911 can only be taken as a pious wish."[9]

The governor and other officials tried to convince Hosie that he should not take the Wei River route into Kansu and suggested other routes to him. However, Hosie insisted upon following the river valley, rightly assuming that the officials wished him to avoid the area because they knew poppies were growing there.[10]

In traveling up the Wei valley, Hosie found that close to

the city farmers tried to conceal the fields of poppies but farther out in the countryside there was no attempt to hide them. In a distance of thirty miles he counted fifty-two fields of poppies. He said the officials of the area could not have been ignorant of their existence, because he met one official traveling the same route and poppy fields were clearly visible from the road. One of the Chinese guards assigned to accompany Hosie told him that the poppy fields then growing in the province were only about one-tenth of the amount grown in recent years. He also said that opium prices had fluctuated enormously because of reduced production and the prohibition on trade with other provinces. When asked why farmers grew poppies in defiance of the strict government measures against them, the man said, "One mou of land will produce opium which will realize seven times the price of wheat grown on the same area; and not only will it realize this larger amount, but it will always find a ready market, and what is of still greater importance to the farmer, ready money."[11]

Prior to the imperial edict there were about 530,000 mou of poppies in Shensi. By 1909 this had been reduced to about 372,695 mou. After the suppression movement it was reported that the drug was still sold in 2,894 shops and 2,602 licenses had been issued to people who were allowed to sell it. It was also reported that the province had 404 opium refuges that had cured 568,055 addicts and still had 370,036 in their care. At the same time it was estimated that there were still 938,091 addicts in the province.[12]

The Rev. Arthur G. Shorrock of the English Baptist Mission in Shensi wrote Hosie about poppy cultivation in the province, "In the Shangchow district a great change is reported this year; but, owing to much bribery, the men sent out to investigate gave false reports to the officials, and in consequence a good deal of opium has escaped detection among the hills away from the big roads." Yet, overall, Shorrock concluded, there had been a "vast change," which was "supported by popular sentiment." He noted that "although the people have incurred great loss by the suppression of opium growing, no [up]risings have yet taken place, at least to any extent. Men have been beaten, numbers have worn the cangue, crops have been destroyed everywhere, and yet the people have suffered it." He gave three reasons for acceptance of the situation: first, the people believed the officials to be earnest in the endeavor; second, "the gentry and better educated people are really in sympathy with the Government, and from patriotic reasons use their influence in the right direction"; and, third, the people as a whole supported the movement as they recognized the dangers of opium.[13]

Hosie traveled into Kansu as far as the city of Lanchow, seeing 595 poppy fields on the way. At Lanchow, Hosie met the governor-general of Kansu-Shensi, Ch'ang Keng, who told him the poppy crop was reduced by some 40 percent.[14] Several British missionaries, including George Andrew of the China Inland Mission, reported to Hosie that cultivation was vastly reduced in the last two years in the great opium-producing regions in the north and northeast parts of the province. However, Hosie reported that Andrew "would not pledge himself to actual figures. He was wise, for I do not think that the Chinese authorities, the Chinese Government, or, indeed, anyone can or will be able to say with any degree of precision what the actual reduction has been here or elsewhere."[15]

The British consul in Kansu, O.R. Coales, wrote to Hosie that in one district of the province 50 percent of the Chinese were thought to be addicts, but Muslims, Tibetans, and Mongols who also lived in the area did not use the drug.[16] Going back to Shensi, Hosie counted 2,036 fields of poppies in the Wei River valley, and even in the heart of the poppy-growing areas in southwest China he had never seen fields as tightly packed with flowers as he did in Kansu. It was on this journey back to the Kansu-Shensi border that

Hosie counted the largest number of poppy fields he saw in one day—707.[17]

The difficulty of suppressing the growth of the poppy was related to Hosie in the account of one such attempt. At the end of May, the prefect of Lanchow had been sent to a district to suppress poppy cultivation because the local magistrate had been unable to do so. Farmers were summoned to meet the prefect at a resthouse, and when they were presented to him, one of them knelt before him and seized him by the legs. The rest of the farmers joined in the attack on the official, who was severely injured and had to seek aid from a nearby China Inland Mission doctor. As a result of the attack, one of the official's assistants was beheaded and another was imprisoned. The magistrate was dismissed, but the farmers continued to grow their poppies.[18]

Following his trip to the northwest, Hosie returned to Peking. In December 1910 he departed to visit the southwestern provinces of Szechwan, Yunnan, and Kweichow, where the poppy was planted in the fall and harvested the following spring. Lacking reliable statistics, Hosie estimated that in 1904 the production of opium in Szechwan was 200,000 piculs, of which 180,000 piculs was consumed in the province and the rest exported, mainly via the Yangtze, to other provinces. According to Hosie's estimate, the opium production of the province was four times the amount imported to China from India annually. Hosie had previously lived in Szechwan for five years and had traveled extensively in the west, south, and central parts of the province, but on this journey he was determined to visit the eastern section, about which he knew little and which was said to produce the largest opium crop in the province. Traveling there he found no poppies and learned that officials had had the crops destroyed in 1909 and 1910, and there had been no further attempt to grow them.[19]

In Wanhsien, south of the Yangtze, Hosie reported that poppies had been grown in two places in 1909-10, but at the time of his journey opium had been entirely suppressed. A missionary who had taken a trip through the area a month before Hosie also reported no poppies. He said, "There were remarkable results, and there could be no doubt that the measures taken by the authorities had been most effective in this part of Szechwan. Farmers, however, still held stocks of seed in anticipation of the stringency being relaxed." The eastern area of the province between Wanhsien and Chungking had formerly produced the greatest amount of opium in Szechwan, and Fuchow was the center of the opium market. In this area there had been strenuous opposition to the suppression measures, and in 1910 a larger than usual crop of opium had been harvested. Journeying up the Yangtze, Hosie remembered that he had visited the same place eight years before and had found the fields completely planted in poppies. Now he saw none. Around the village of Ch'ichiang on the Szechwan-Kweichow border, where Hosie had seen extensive poppy fields in 1882, he now found none. The results were the same in other areas where he had observed poppies in 1882 and 1903. Both missionaries and Chinese officials assured him there were no poppies in the province. Leaving the province Hosie noted, "I had now spent sixty-six days in Szechwan, once the greatest opium-producing province in China, and, in spite of careful investigation, had not found a single poppy plant."[20]

From Szechwan Hosie traveled to Yunnan, where after a fortnight he wrote, "My quest of the poppy had been fruitless." Then, in the city of Tungch'uan, Yunnan, Hosie was told that poppies had been seen in bloom the previous week in one or two places to the southwest of the city. He immediately set out to see for himself and encountered some of the most difficult terrain of his journey. On the second day out of the city, he came to a high plateau ideally suited for poppy cultivation. The people there told him they had planted poppies the previous autumn, but in January officials had forced them to uproot the crop. Then, in a remote mountain valley, Hosie found four plots of poppies from which opium was being harvested. One plot was twenty by five yards and the others were about twice that size, but the crop looked quite inferior. On a six-day journey on side roads, Hosie counted sixty-three plots of poppies, "an indication of the conditions prevailing in the remoter parts of the province." Yet Hosie noted that at a place where in 1882 he reported that two-thirds of the valley had been in poppies there were now none. He also reported that "native opium in Yunnan was now worth exactly its weight in silver or about six times its value in 1906."[21]

For Yunnan, Hosie estimated the pre-1906 production at about 60,000 piculs. The opium of the province was considered the best produced in China and was often adulterated with lower quality Szechwan opium. In the main opium-producing districts of the province he found cultivation had been suppressed, but in the remoter regions of the west he found a total of seventy-two plots. He thought this was also the case in other more remote sections of the eastern part of the province, which he did not visit, and noted that "it is true that raw opium could be purchased secretly at most places along the road I traveled, but that the supply is derived from old stocks held by private individuals, who employ friends and agents to dispose of it retail." He estimated that by 1910-11 the production of the province had decreased by about 75 percent. Hosie credited Hsi-liang, the viceroy of Yunnan-Kweichow from 1907 to 1909, with the suppression of much of the cultivation. Hsi-liang had proclaimed that cultivation of the poppy had to cease by 21 January 1909 and that no opium would be allowed to pass a customs station or likin barrier after 21 September 1908. The viceroy, Li Ching-hsi, who came to the province in 1910, had, after repeated refusals, finally allowed opium to be exported to Tongking in 1911.[22]

From Yunnan, Hosie went to Kweichow, where, stopping for the night at an official resthouse, he wrote he had seen

Lower-class opium smokers reclining on sawhorses and planks. Arthur E. Moule, *New China and Old*, 1902.

no poppies that day, "but I was not long in smelling opium fumes . . . and I found it necessary to put a stop to the smoking of two of my porters, who were all guaranteed non-smokers when we started from Yunnan-fu!"[23]

In Kweichow in 1882 and 1883 Hosie had seen vast amounts of poppies growing in the narrow valleys of the province. In one high valley, where he had observed that 90 percent of the crop in 1882 was poppies, he now saw only three stray plants, "proof that stringent measures had been taken to suppress cultivation." Yet the suppression effort had not been uniform. At one place he saw part of a field planted in poppies, the rest of which had evidently been destroyed, and a second field that had not been tampered with. In other places poppies grew undisturbed.[24]

The area around Longtait'ing had been the best opium-producing area in Kweichow, but its importance had been diminished as a result of the prohibition edict. Hosie found one field of poppies in a village where the people told him the poppy had been completely suppressed two years earlier, but when they learned it still grew in a neighboring district, they too had replanted it. Then in December, January, and March their fields had been raided and the crop destroyed by officials. Hosie reported that the raids had not been totally effective because he saw some fields partially destroyed, while adjoining ones had not been touched. In the district, he counted sixty-seven plots still containing poppies.[25]

In a conversation with the governor of Kweichow, P'ang Hung-shu, Hosie was told that poppy cultivation was diminished about 70 to 80 percent and that it would be eradicated the following year. The best estimates were that Kweichow produced 40,000 to 50,000 piculs a year prior to 1906, but the opium of the region was quite inferior to that of Yunnan and Szechwan. While Hsi-liang took no direct role in the suppression movement in Kweichow, leaving the matter entirely to the provincial authorities, the stringent proclamations, repeatedly issued, had been mostly ignored by the farmers. In February and March 1911 troops were sent out to uproot the crops; sometimes they met with resistance, such as the skirmish between troops and Miao-tze tribesmen who were growing opium, in which about a hundred of the latter were killed. In twenty-nine days of travel in the province, Hosie counted 211 fields of poppies.[26]

Hosie wrote, in conclusion, that in 1910 poppy cultivation was eradicated in Shansi and reduced 30 percent in Shensi and 25 percent in Kansu, compared with 1907. Cultivation had ceased in Szechwan and was reduced by 75 percent in Yunnan and 70 percent in Kweichow. "This was, on the whole," he noted, "a notable achievement which was, however, nullified by the outbreak of the revolution in October 1911 when the Central and Provincial Governments lost control and were unable, for the time being, to prevent a recrudescence of poppy cultivation."[27]

As Hosie's findings had vividly illustrated, the success of the opium suppression movement in any area depended upon the actions of the officials. In Szechwan the suppression was very effective, largely because of the efforts of the officials, Hsi-liang, Chao Erh-hsun, and his brother and successor, Chao Erh-feng. Just prior to leaving the province in May 1907, Hsi-liang had written, "Opium suppression is the foundation on which China is seeking wealth and power, and everyone, including officials, local elite, and the masses must know this; going forward with their full strength and determination, they will be able to achieve it."[28]

The British ambassador in China, Sir John N. Jordan, wrote that Chao Erh-hsun "had done more than any other man to rid his country of opium." Chao had told Jordan "that the knowledge that British eyes were watching and British observers reporting on the progress of the opium campaign in every corner of the province had served as a great stimulus to himself and his subordinates to carry on the struggle to the finish."[29]

It was particularly significant that Szechwan had been able to eliminate the poppy, which in the latter years of the nineteenth century had become increasingly important in the economy of the province. Because of its location, Szechwan was a major trading center, but in the 1890s several factors began to alter the trading patterns. Increasing imports to China of kerosene oil resulted in a sharp decline in the demand for candle wax, which had been a major export of the province. The demand for vegetable dyes, long an important export, declined as chemical dyes from the West began reaching the Chinese coastal cities. Into these gaps opium quickly moved.[30] Although Hosie thought there was popular support in Szechwan for the suppression movement,

a British consul told him he thought the farmers were in-
different or hostile to the movement.[31] Others thought that
instead of direct protest against the opium suppression
movement there was increased participation in antigovern-
ment organizations, such as the Railway League. Some
people in Szechwan thought the success of the 1911 revolution meant they were free to do as they pleased with regard
to planting opium.[32] At the International Opium Conference at The Hague, the Chinese delegate T'ang Kuo-an
commented upon a report in the London *Times* that attributed the revolutionary movement to the revival of opium
cultivation, stating that "if this was true, it was only a re-
grettable incident of the present situation, and that when
order was re-established, the Chinese Government would
pursue its anti-opium measures with still greater energy
than before."[33]

In Yunnan, Hsi-liang was much more strict in his program for opium suppression than was required by the central government. All officials there were required to quit
smoking immediately. Persons not holding official posts
were given one year to stop the habit or face prosecution by
the state.[34] This requirement that officials quit smoking
immediately was also adopted in other provinces, with the
result that some officials died from sudden withdrawal of
the drug. General Ma Yu-k'un, commander-in-chief of
northern forces at Pakou, Chihli, was "one of the noted
victims of the anti-opium regulations. Addicted to the smoking of the drug, he made a manful attempt to obey Imperial behests to break off the habit. But it proved too much
even for so strong a man as he was, and he died at
T'ungchow in the fall of 1907."[35]

But all officials charged with opium suppression were
not so vigorous and many were themselves addicted to the
drug. As one Westerner noted, "the private squeeze from
the trade, especially when it became illicit, is of course, one
of the most elastic sources of income for the unscrupulous

official, and he was under the strongest temptation to become a partner in the traffic."[36]

The unevenness of the suppression movement was evident in many reports. In March 1908 the *Chinese Recorder* published replies to a circular sent to missionaries in various parts of the country. Few replies were received from the far southwestern provinces, but of the others about four-fifths replied affirmatively to the question, "Has the anti-opium edict been posted?" There had been more delays in posting the edict in the central provinces, and from Hupeh it was reported that officials had taken no action to have the edict made public. Asked if the move to close opium dens had been successful, those from Manchuria, Shantung, Kiangsu, Hunan, Chekiang, and Fukien reported that all dens had been closed, but a few missionaries noted that some illicit dens were still operating. Provinces reporting partial success in closing dens were Chihli and Anhwei. The effort was said to be unsuccessful in Kwangtung, Honan, and Hupeh. Regarding Honan, it was reported that "no honest attempt appeared to have been made by the high officials to enforce the edict," and in Hupeh "high officials seem to have ignored the edicts, and such success as has occurred in parts has been due to the action of local officials." To the question asking if there were any attempt to stop the sale of opium in shops, replies from Manchuria, Chihli, Kiangsu, and Fukien were that only officially licensed shops were allowed to sell the drug. Provinces reporting sales as usual were Shantung, Anhwei, Honan, Hupeh, Hunan, Chekiang, and Kwangtung. Regarding the reduction of poppy cultivation, the reports from Anhwei and Manchuria said all cultivation was forbidden; Chihli, Kiangsu, Chekiang, Shantung, Honan, and Fukien reported great reductions; Hunan and Hupeh reported there had been no reduction. There was no report on cultivation from Kwangtung.[37]

Opium refuges had been opened in some provinces as a result of the suppression movement. Manchuria, Shantung, Honan, Chekiang, and Kwangtung each reported having one refuge. There were refuges in Chihli, but the missionaries reported that anti-opium pills and morphia were preferred methods of curing addiction there. Kiangsu had refuges in Shanghai, Soochow, Chinkiang, and Hwaian, and Anhwei had several in various cities. Hupeh had no refuges, but one was said to be in the planning stages at Hankow. From Fukien came the report that the magistrate was attempting to cure forty addicts per month but had not yet been successful. Asked if the suppression movement were a popular one (involving the gentry and the people) and if the official attitude were zealous, most missionaries reported the movement did have support among the gentry and the people. Yet, negative comments included, "there is opium-smoking among the officials and consequently no zeal," "some officials are zealous, but the Prefect is an opium smoker," and "officials [are] the reverse of zealous." Only from Hupeh did all the reports say there was no popular movement and the officials were uninterested in the reform. More difficult to answer was the question were the Chinese making any attempt to influence public opinion regarding the opium suppression campaign. The missionaries' conclusion was that "public opinion in China is of so recent a growth, and the idea of educating it along moral lines so novel, that nothing systematic other than the posting of the edicts has been attempted."[38]

The conclusions of the reports were that opium suppression was most successful in the coastal provinces and less successful in the central provinces. It was also acknowledged that "the power of the official class to make or unmake the movement is evident and the fact that opium-smoking still largely obtains among this class, is one of the depressing features of the situation."[39]

BRITISH DIPLOMATS AND THE END OF THE TRADE FROM INDIA

The British documentation on the ending of the opium trade is enormous. British officials in China sent numerous reports to their ambassador in Peking and to London on the progress of opium reform, particularly after the 1907 agreement to reduce the trade from India to China. As previously noted, the British took the position that China had to be entirely free from all native opium before the export of the drug from India would cease. It is important to note that the 1907 agreement only called for the British to reduce the export of opium from India. It was up to the Chinese to control the import of the drug to their country. The Chinese took the position that once an area of China was free from the drug, they had the right to demand that the importation of Indian opium to that area cease. Determining where opium was and was not growing in China and where the importation of the drug from India was and was not permitted by Chinese authorities became extremely complicated as the suppression movement continued.

Because of the differences in the interpretations of the 1907 agreement, disputes between the Chinese and the British quite naturally arose. Both sides hoped to resolve disputes when on 8 May 1911, the British minister, Sir John N. Jordan, and the president of the *Wai-wu Pu* (Foreign Office), Tsou Chia-lai, signed a further agreement intended to cover the seven remaining years of the original 1907 agreement. Jordan wrote to Sir Edward Grey, Britain's foreign minister, that the new agreement recognized "the signal success which has so far attended the Chinese efforts to suppress the growth of native opium, and, as a token of their readiness to facilitate the continuance of this work and to ensure its ultimate consummation."[40]

During the negotiations of the new agreement several major diplomatic problems regarding prohibition of the foreign drug and the stocks of the drug then in China arose. The Chinese insisted on banning the import of Indian opium on a province-by-province basis as domestic cultivation was curtailed. Jordan wrote to Grey that agreeing to this proposal would create a major problem in the coastal provinces; they produced little native opium, and if the Chinese suppressed that small amount they would be free to demand the exclusion of the foreign drug from these areas. This would mean that Canton and Shanghai, as well as other treaty ports located in the coastal provinces, could legally be closed to the drug, stopping the opium trade entirely. A second problem concerned the stocks of opium then in the warehouses of the treaty ports. The Chinese were demanding that all opium coming from India be certified before entering China so that the amount could be carefully controlled. They insisted they were not responsible for the stocks of the drug then in the treaty ports, while the British pointed out that the stocks were there because of Chinese demand for the drug. The most the Chinese would offer on this point was to allow existing stocks to make up some of the yearly quota allowed to be imported from India.[41] This matter of the existing stocks in China was to plague the British minister for many months to come.

The 1911 agreement called for continuing the reduction of the opium trade so that it would cease entirely by 1917 or before that date if the Chinese could prove that all native cultivation had stopped (Article 1). Jordan noted that the movement against opium was not uniform throughout China, and in accordance with this situation the agreement provided "that Indian opium shall not enter any province which can establish clear evidence that it has effectively suppressed the cultivation and import of native opium. It is understood, however, that the closing of the ports of Canton and Shanghai . . . shall not take effect except as the final step" of the program (Articles 2 and 3). British officials, accompanied by Chinese officials if they so desired, were permitted to make investigations in the Chinese provinces to determine if domestic cultivation were being curtailed (Article 4). The Chinese were allowed to send an official to India to watch the export of opium (Article 5). A uniform tax of 350 taels per 100-catty chest was levied on domestic opium (Article 6), and all restrictions imposed by provincial authorities on the wholesale trade of Indian opium were to be withdrawn and all duties consolidated in the import duty (Article 7). Opium exported from India to China was to be accompanied by a certificate so that the amount could be controlled to meet the yearly reductions necessary for the trade to end by 1917 (Article 8). The final article permitted the revision of the agreement with the consent of both parties.[42]

This 1911 agreement was to cause many problems. In their zeal to suppress opium in their country, the Chinese, particularly some local officials, often took actions that were now illegal. In a message to Prince Ch'ing on 7 September 1911, Jordan pointed out several instances of breaches of the treaty. He cited Fukien, where local officials had imposed anti-opium regulations in violation of both the Chefoo Agreement and the 1911 agreement. Also, local officials there were seizing opium that did not have the license they required. Hunan officials also required purchasers of imported raw opium to pay a smokers' license tax, and a local tax was being levied against Chinese opium, although such taxes were prohibited by the agreement.[43]

The problem of local restrictions on imported Indian opium increasingly concerned the British diplomatic representatives as the Chinese became more determined in their efforts to rid the country of opium. There were numerous breaches of the 1911 agreement, which the British repeatedly pointed out to the Chinese. It should be noted that many firms engaged in the business of importing Indian opium to China and did not wish to see the trade end, hence, they were very unhappy with the Chinese move to suppress the use of opium. Members of the Sassoon family were most vocal in protesting to British officials every attempt by the Chinese to stop the trade. Quite often they were disappointed by the lack of vigor on the part of the consular officials to whom they complained, and they frequently resorted to appeals to more senior officials in London.

Opium belonging to the Sassoons was seized by Chinese officials at Amoy in March 1911 and a second shipment was taken the following month. At least part of the problem was that all opium shipped from India was to be certified by the government there before it left for China, and frequently the Sassoons' ships carried uncertified opium, which Chinese officials rightfully seized once the ships reached a Chinese port. The Sassoons also had trouble trying to sell the stocks they were holding in China at the time the 1911 agreement took effect.[44]

British officials could not ignore the numerous protests from the Sassoons and usually tried to get the Chinese to return the confiscated opium to the merchants. Quite frequently, the Sassoons demanded both payment for the opium and punitive compensation for their losses, but they were lucky if they succeeded in getting the opium returned. One of these seizures of Sassoon-owned opium led the British to take more drastic action. The incident began when E.D. and David Sassoon, on behalf of their companies, informed the foreign office on 23 September 1912 that "Anking authorities have forcibly seized and destroyed by fire seven cases Malwa opium taken from China Merchants' Steam Navigation Company's hulk. Such oppressive and high-handed measures have caused utmost consternation amongst all dealers and merchants, and we respectfully request prompt protective action."[45] On the 24th, Jordan informed Grey that "continued representations to the Central Government have hitherto proved futile, and I would propose, subject to your approval, to send His Majesty's consul-general at Shanghai in a man-of-war to Anking, which is the capital of Anhwei and not an open port, to investigate this case on the spot." India Office reports indicated that as a result of the Anhwei incident and regulations imposed by officials there the "opium market [is] said to be demoralized." Grey approved the action Jordan suggested on 28 September and the foreign office informed the Sassoons of the planned action.[46]

Consul Sir Everard H. Fraser of Shanghai sailed for Anking on the gunboat *Flora* on 2 October 1912. In meeting with the local official, Pai, who had seized the opium, Fraser quickly realized that the official was ignorant of the provisions of the 1911 agreement and the fact that the Republican government had agreed to abide by it. Both the official and his chief assistant were quite disturbed by the visit of the British consul once they realized their own actions were in violation of international treaties. The whole visit seems comical in retrospect, since the Chinese official was unsure of the proper protocol for dealing with a visiting British official, and, after the first meeting, retreated behind the excuse that he had "a cold due to the sudden change of temperatures." He recovered his health when he finally learned what was expected of him from an American missionary with whom he was on friendly terms. During the three days the Chinese official was suffering from his cold, the captain of the *Flora* "insisted that the unusual lowness of the water, which was falling steadily, rendered it imperative" that the British sail without delay. Fortunately for Fraser, the Chinese official recovered before the British found themselves stranded by the receding waters, and at another meeting Pai told Fraser that "the matter was beyond his province, and he had therefore sent a full report to his Government, whose instructions, whatever might be their tenor, he would carry out scrupulously." Fraser observed that the action of Pai "appeared to me not without cleverness," because "he could tell his provincial assembly and the native public that his well-meant efforts to eradicate the vice had been thwarted by his superiors at the bidding of Great Britain, whereas if he yielded to my representations he would have to confess that he had acted ill-advisedly." Fraser continued that "Pai is a genuine fanatic on the subject of opium, inexperienced in government administration and ignorant of the treaty stipulations, and owing probably to his sojourn at a military college in Japan, imbued with the belief that China has been the victim of foreign aggression, from which it is a patriot's duty to free her." Fraser thought "the appearance of His Majesty's ship, *Flora*, undoubtedly had a good effect on" the Chinese. Officials of the central government later tried to defend and explain the actions of the Anking officials, but they refused to pay compensation for the opium. Still, Jordan believed sending the gunboat had been beneficial, since the Chinese realized the British were determined not to tolerate repeated treaty violations.[47]

To comply with the 1911 agreement, inspections to determine the extent of domestic poppy cultivation were necessary and several were made, but none were as extensive as Hosie's had been. The British minister Jordan listed the places where the foreign drug was prohibited once it was proven that they were free of native cultivation. Reports of these investigations were similar to the one from Consul-General H.E. Fulford in Tientsin on the actions of Chihli officials in suppressing opium in the spring of 1911. They had issued instructions for stopping the use of the drug within two years. The two years were divided into eight periods of three months each, during which opium prevention committees were to be organized, smokers were to be identified and placed on lists, preparations were to be made for breaking the habit among the smokers, all shops selling opium were to be closed, addicts were to give up the drug, all establishments that helped addicts break the habit were to be disbanded, final measures were to be taken to make sure the habit had been eradicated, and the central bureau was to make an investigation of the work and report to the viceroy. Fulford noted that the instructions were thorough and that no one was to be excluded because of age. As part of the final measures to make sure the opium habit had been eradicated, all private opium stocks were to be surrendered under threat of heavy penalties, and informers were to be rewarded.[48]

In sending this report to Grey, Jordan noted that what was being done in Chihli was fairly typical of other provinces and two years was generally the length of time set for the anti-opium campaign. He wrote, "It is considered impossible to keep up the popular enthusiasm for a longer period, and, rather than admit failure the Chinese Government and the Chinese people are evidently determined to incur any sacrifice, however great." He continued that in the next two years he expected to "see the most drastic methods applied to opium suppression, and neither treaties nor other considerations will, I fear, receive much attention if they are found to stand in the way of the great reform on which this country is now fairly embarked."[49]

The collapse of the Ch'ing dynasty and the coming to power of the new Republican government altered the opium suppression campaign in some ways, but again it depended upon the local officials whether or not the campaign was successful. Officials in London suggested to Jordan that they might ask for a promise from the Republican government to continue opium suppression as a requirement for recognition of the new government. Jordan was opposed to this idea, because, he said, the 1911 agreement had been worked out with the greatest difficulty and in opposition to the wishes of many Chinese who wanted the opium trade to stop immediately. He acknowledged that opium was again being grown in some provinces where the foreign drug was banned, but "it appears to me that the less opium is brought into the question of recognition the better it will be for British prestige and British interests in China."[50]

As further evidence of the difficulty the opium issue might cause, he enclosed with his report an undated item from the Peking *Daily News,* which said one of the responsibilities of the Chinese people in building a "new national life is the strong, vigorous movement against the opium habit," because "the curse of opium has brought ruin and sorrow to [the] land." The article continued that the 1911 agreement with the British was more favorable to the opium traders than it was to the Chinese, and asked, "Can such a condition continue under the Republic of China? No! is the reply of the Republican officials and the people alike." It suggested that the way to rid China of the opium evil was by "strong public action by the Government, so that the world may know that it is the real desire and determination of the new republic to end this source of weakness and ruin in China. The people will earnestly support this strong moral appeal by the Government, that in the name of humanity this evil trade may stop." The article went on to note that Christians in Britain would help the Chinese. It said, "The citizens of this great nation feel as never before that the opium habit is a disgrace to the republic and it must go." The article concluded by quoting two British missionaries, J. Hudson Taylor, who wrote, "Ah! we have given China something besides the Gospel, something that is doing more harm in a week than the united efforts of all our Christians are doing good in a year. Oh, the evils of opium!" and Arnold Foster, who wrote, "Indian opium . . . has poured into China a never-ceasing stream of poison all through the Victorian era. Ours have been and are the profits, ours is the sin."[51] Eventually, the British recognized the republican government without tying the recognition to the matter of opium suppression. However, the new government agreed to abide by the 1911 agreement and others concerning opium.

Reports of the recrudescence of poppy cultivation after the 1911 revolution began to be received from British officials in various regions of China. From Yunnan on 9 February 1912, H.W. Gammon reported that the poppy was again being grown in the province. He indicated that the military governor had recently issued a proclamation prohibiting the cultivation of the poppy and the sale of the drug. However, Gammon thought the proclamation was "merely an obvious and hypocritical pretense on the part of the provincial authorities in consideration of recent opium agreements with foreign Powers, to carry on the work of suppression begun by his Excellency Hsi-liang and continued by the ex-Viceroy." Another report, on 6 June 1912, said that poppies were numerous along the railroad from Haiphong to Yunnanfu.[52]

Consul P.E. O'Brien-Butler reported on 25 June that the production in Yunnan was then four-fifths what it had been prior to the 1906 prohibition. He said that the local government had attempted to buy the entire crop at thirty cents a Chinese ounce but that the amount the officials were able to purchase was quite small. It had been their intention to sell the drug in Tongking, but the farmers found others willing to buy it secretly at sixty-five to seventy-five cents an ounce. In reporting to Grey on 6 January 1913, Jordan wrote that cultivation of the poppy was increasing dramatically in Yunnan, and D.J. Harding of the China Inland Mission at Chuching had written that people in the area did not want opium suppression and that he had been cursed in the markets by people because he was from England, "'that country that is compelling China to give up the opium,' and only a few months ago one of the authorities told me that what they wanted was that England should leave them alone to deal with the matter as they think best."[53] From Szechwan,

Consul Wilkinson reported on 10 January 1912 that farmers who had lost money in the railway venture were planting poppies to recoup their losses. He reported that the government in Chengtu had issued a circular stating opium eradication was necessary to strengthen China and that there would be severe punishments for anyone who grew poppies. In 1913, it was reported that poppies were being cultivated in at least two districts in Szechwan but that officials had demanded that they be destroyed.[54]

In February 1912 Jordan wrote Grey that in a conversation with Yuan Shih-k'ai on the 20th he "took the opportunity of remarking on the recrudescence of opium cultivation, and his Excellency gave me to understand that as soon as peace and order were restored this, like many other matters, would not be lost sight of." The republican government did try to continue the opium suppression movement. Shortly after speaking to Jordan, Yuan issued an order noting that while restrictions against opium had recently been relaxed by some officials, they were now instructed to renew their suppression efforts. He wrote, "The abolition of opium is intended to save the people and free them from a grievous danger. . . . Suppression should not be overlooked for the sake of a temporary gain." Sun Yat-sen in March 1912 urged that the people not relax their efforts to rid China of opium. He said, "Those who consume this poison for sensual pleasure, and besotted and stupid, refuse to reform, cannot be regarded as citizens of the republic." He recommended that the new government adopt laws banning opium addicts from the privileges of citizenship.[55]

Although the British were disturbed that opium was again being grown in the provinces where the Indian drug was prohibited, it was not long a problem for the British. The British and Indian firms engaged in the opium trade continued to have difficulty selling the stocks already in their warehouses in China. As the Republican government did not have complete control over the provinces of China, the merchants realized that the British diplomatic officials would have only limited success in resolving difficulties the merchants had with local officials concerning opium. Unwilling to risk trying to sell their opium under such conditions, the foreign merchants asked the British to stop selling opium in India for the China market. On 31 December 1912, W. Langley of the foreign office notified the Sassoons that the Indian government was being asked "that the Government sales of opium . . . be postponed until the position in China improves."[56]

Meanwhile the Sassoons continued to complain that they were unable to get rid of their enormous stock of opium already in China. They tried to convince Grey to pressure the Chinese government to buy up their stocks, so that their monetary loss would not be so great. Grey refused. Much of the opium in the warehouses had been bought on speculation that the price in China would increase as the Chinese curtailed their domestic production. The merchants failed to realize that the Chinese people were indeed determined to suppress the use of the drug in China and that there would be no demand for the stockpiled opium.[57]

But the opium firms were not the only ones who were hurt by the suppression movement. The situation put many of the foreign banking firms in jeopardy because they had financed the speculative buying. Chekiang officials had issued a prohibition against Indian opium in February 1912, and in June the managers of eleven Shanghai banks, led by the Chartered Bank of India, Australia, and China and the Hongkong and Shanghai Banking Corporation, wrote to British officials that the situation was becoming critical. They said that native opium was prevalent in Chekiang and was openly sold in Shanghai and that the prohibition of Indian opium was "in absolute contravention of existing treaties." The stocks in the warehouses were increasing and the value of the opium was declining as a result of this illegal action. Because of the action of the Chekiang officials,

"the opium market has been paralysed, the merchants having been unable to move off their stocks and repay the
money the banks have advanced to them and should the
present state of affairs be allowed to continue, disastrous
failures may result involving the banks in heavy losses." The
amount of money tied up in the opium stocks was several
millions of pounds.[58]

In December 1912, the Sassoons protested to British officials that all of China was closed to imported opium except
for the port of Shanghai, even though the exclusion was a
violation of the 1911 agreement. Opium merchants in Hong
Kong were urging that the sale of certified opium for China
be stopped. At the end of January 1913, the Chinese foreign minister asked Jordan to have his government stop the
sale of opium bound for Chinese ports. By May, Jordan was
suggesting to London that the 1911 agreement be revised in
view of the current conditions in China, and before the summer ended the agreement was canceled and the export from
India of opium bound for China had ceased.[59]

The opium problem was not settled, however, because the
foreign opium merchants in China still had huge stocks of
the drug of which to dispose. Several suggestions were en-
tertained. At one point, the Chinese government offered
to buy it for sale through the government opium monopolies. Later, the Chinese withdrew this offer but said they
would pay the freight if the merchants would remove the
opium from China. Interestingly, the opium merchants had
been looking for several months into the possibility of selling the surplus opium in Mexico. Then, in early 1914, the
republican government again offered to buy the stocks for
the express purpose of publicly burning it once the trans-
action was completed. Jordan took a dim view of this idea.
He noted that the Chinese government was in severe financial difficulties and that the Chinese people were not likely
to silently accept the expenditure of £6 million (the cur-

rent value of the stocks) for opium to be burned. He doubted the Chinese would be able to pay, and if the British pressed the Chinese for payment they would gain no friends. Jordan concluded his message to Grey, "We seem so far as I can see, to have reached a stage in the history of the opium question when we must either make a virtue of a necessity and remove stocks, which I venture to think ought never to have been sent, or risk national dishonor by ending the opium traffic in a holocaust at the expense of China."[60]

The government of India had been requested as early as June 1912 to stop the trade, but sales continued until 1913, with an additional 10,863 chests reaching China during that period. Jordan was furious that the trade had been allowed to continue that long. He asked Grey how the British government could consent to the provisions of The Hague Convention and at the same time allow the trade from India to continue. Regarding the opium in the warehouses in China, Jordan wrote, "The Chinese know as well as we do that we dare not in the last resort enforce our opium treaties, and the situation is an undignified one which reacts unfavorably on all our relations with China." He continued that "the spontaneous withdrawal of the stocks would produce an excellent impression and would go far towards removing the feelings of resentment and soreness which now exist in the minds of the Chinese. It would be a just and generous act which would form a fitting end to a trade which has become a moral anachronism." He further noted that if the British prolong the "sales and extract the last farthing from the traffic, we shall certainly go down in Chinese history as a people who ended as we began, by forcing opium upon China. The end, if generous, will do much to obliterate the remembrance of the past and to remove the only blot which has stained our reputation in the Far East." Jordan wanted the Indian government to take back the stocks and treat them as exports to non-Chinese markets, and he was strongly opposed to asking the Chinese to help pay the cost of transporting the stocks out of China.[61] Because less than two years earlier Jordan had ordered a gunboat to Anhwei to protest the seizure of foreign-owned opium, some people in the British government thought he had "entirely lost his balance and . . . became absolutely pro-Chinese" on the matter of the opium stocks.[62]

The problem of the opium stocks was not easily resolved. Some of it was sold to an opium monopoly in Hong Kong, whence quantities were later smuggled into China and the United States. By 1915, the Chinese government had quietly purchased some of the stocks for resale through the government opium monopolies, and eventually another monopoly purchased the remaining stocks for resale in Kiangsu, Kiangsi, and Kwangtung. There still remained a problem of the opium stocks at Shanghai, which were eventually sold to a Chinese monopoly there. Grey wrote to Jordan that the consul in Shanghai, Sir Everard H. Fraser, who had gone to Anking on the gunboat, had suggested the solution to the problem was to "make it a criminal offense for any British subject to have any interest in opium" after 31 March 1917.[63] Later that year in Britain, the Society for the Suppression of the Opium Trade formally disbanded, but not before appointing a Vigilance Committee.[64]

The official opium trade in which the British government of India had engaged for a century had ended without fanfare. The opium suppression campaign in China had not been a complete success, but it had aroused the Chinese to the point where they would no longer tolerate foreign opium being sold in their country. At the beginning of the opium suppression movement, many people had noted that if the suppression were to be a reality, it would have to be done quickly, because the fervor of the people could not be sustained for a very long time. As it turned out, the suppression campaign was most successful in those areas where there was strong support for it among the officials who were charged with carrying out the orders of the central government. In those areas where officials relied on the reports of others or took little or no interest in the campaign, poppies continued to grow and opium continued to be used as it had for many years. If sometimes the Chinese officials became overzealous in their efforts, they might be excused on the grounds that opium was an issue about which few Chinese did not hold strong opinions in the early years of the twentieth century. The Chinese had embarked upon a vast program of social reform, which they had decided their country needed. The national mood regarding opium was such that they were not willing to tolerate protests over the niceties of treaty provisions, particularly from the British, who had brought opium to China a century earlier, creating the problem.

If the British and other foreigners had been skeptical in their views of the possibility for Chinese success in the program when it began in 1906, they soon had to admit that many Chinese were indeed determined to eradicate opium from China once and for all. The task was not impossible, as the case of Szechwan had proved, but it was difficult. The recrudescence of poppy cultivation in China was most evident in those areas where the republican government had the most difficulty with other matters as well. The remote parts of southwestern China, long the largest opium-producing regions of the country, were the ones where the republican government had little influence. With no strong central government to insist upon continued opium suppression and local officials who did not press for it, farmers soon began growing poppies again. Despite the best efforts of the Chinese government both before and after the 1911 revolution, opium was still available for purchase either through the government opium monopoly or illegally from private stocks, and addicts were still numerous enough that there was a demand for the drug once domestic production resumed. The suppression campaign had not been completely successful, long-lived, or widespread enough to eliminate opium addiction. And since some demand remained, production soon resumed to meet it.

Conclusion

Opium was an evil that had long sapped the strength of China. By the late nineteenth century many people realized how physically debilitating the constant use of the drug was. Earlier in the century many people had defended the use of the drug by the Chinese on the grounds that physiologically the Chinese were different from other people and that, consequently, they needed the drug to sustain life. Such statements illustrated the lack of medical knowledge about the true nature of opium, which had beneficial uses if properly controlled but had disastrous effects when used indiscriminately. Largely through the work of the missionary doctors, medical evidence was accumulated that dispelled many of the commonly held beliefs about opium, including that it protected the user against malaria or other diseases. The Chinese had long recognized the dangers of the drug. They said that if one were suffering from an illness and opium was prescribed as a cure, as was frequently the case, the person shortly had not only the original illness, still uncured, but also the opium habit.

The Protestant missionaries in China were among the first people to actively and fervently campaign against the use of the drug. Opium addicts were untrustworthy and hence banned from church membership. With so many Chinese automatically excluded from the possibility of conversion, missionaries began to campaign against the drug. Also, the missionaries were concerned with reforming Chinese society, particularly with regard to those customs, such as footbinding, which they viewed as uncivilized, and as a part of this general campaign to change China they sought to eliminate the use of opium. The missionaries were most successful not in convincing the Chinese to give up the drug but in keeping the issue before the public in Britain and finally in getting the British government to admit the error of its involvement in the drug trade. For the missionaries and their allies, the struggle against opium was long and difficult. The Society for the Suppression of the Opium Trade was founded in 1874, but it was not until 1891 that it was able to get the Parliament to adopt a resolution calling the trade "morally indefensible." But getting the Parliament to adopt a resolution and actually stopping the trade were not the same. Not until 1907, after the issuance of the Chinese edict banning the use of the drug, did the British government take further action to curtail its involvement in the opium trade. And in 1913, it was not missionaries but the opium merchants who asked that the trade from India be stopped.

The missionaries faced several problems in their campaign against opium. They knew the harm the drug did, and the missionary doctors were gathering evidence to prove their point medically, but they had difficulties convincing people both in Britain and in China that they were right about opium. To Englishmen, if opium were a problem in China, that was a Chinese problem. In China, the missionaries faced a difficult challenge. Despite all the energy the missionaries expended, only when the Chinese finally recognized the harm opium did to their people did they take action to suppress it. If the missionaries did not eliminate opium from China or stop the trade from India, it was not because they did not try but rather because they recognized the evils of the drug too soon, at a time when others were not yet ready to accept what they said. The role of the missionaries was one of publicist: constantly keeping the issue before the British government until it was forced to take action.

The time and conditions in China were right in 1906 for opium suppression. Many Chinese had long recognized the dangers of the drug, but widescale efforts to eradicate its use came only as a part of the reform movement of the late Ch'ing dynasty. Even though the Chinese produced more of the drug than was imported from India by the turn of the twentieth century, opium was associated in the minds of most Chinese with foreigners and foreign domination. In the milieu of emerging Chinese nationalism, the campaign against opium, begun in 1906, proved quite successful. It was one reform that everyone could understand and the results of which were evident to all. There was nothing abstract about opium reform. If the illiterate worker could not understand the intricacies of other reforms proposed and implemented at this time, he could understand what opium suppression meant. It was this wide appeal that made the campaign as successful as it was.

Ironically, it was opium that brought the Chinese to an international conference as an equal rather than as a defeated nation for the first time. It was also the recognition by the Chinese that other nations, too, had drug problems that allowed the Chinese to face their own problem realistically. The international conferences were called because the Western nations realized that harmful drugs had to be controlled, and these meetings coincided with the passage of drug laws in many nations. At the international conference in Shanghai in 1909, the Chinese realized for the first time that if they were sincere in their desire to rid their country of opium the other nations of the world were willing to commit themselves to helping China by regulating the international trade of drugs. And Britain, particularly, indicated willingness to help China eradicate opium in 1907 when it agreed to decrease the export of opium from India to correspond with the decline of domestic production in China.

But in the end, it was individual efforts on the part of many Chinese that made opium suppression the most successful of the reforms of the late Ch'ing dynasty. The individual addict had to suffer through the agony of breaking the habit. The individual official had to risk the displeasure, and not infrequently the physical abuse, of farmers and opium merchants whose incomes depended upon the drug. And they, in turn, each had to face the problem of finding another means of livelihood. To anyone, Chinese or foreign, who was skeptical in 1906 about the Chinese desire to eradicate opium, proof was not long in coming. True, opium suppression was not uniform throughout China, but in some areas it was successful enough to convince even the most hardened skeptic that the Chinese really were determined to rid their country of the drug that had plagued them for so long.

Perhaps complete suppression of a social evil is never possible in any society. In the case of China in the first decade of the twentieth century, there really was not enough time to learn if opium could be entirely suppressed. The elimination of the drug from the once poppy-covered province of Szechwan certainly proved that eradication was not an impossibility. But before there was time to discover if the use of the drug and the cultivation of the poppy could be completely eradicated, the 1911 revolution intervened, bringing new problems to China. Certainly the inability of the republican government to control the major opium-producing provinces of the southwest contributed to the recrudescence of poppy cultivation. China had come close to being free of opium in 1911, but the campaign wavered under the new republican government. It was many long years before another government of China would try again to eradicate opium. The successes of the suppression campaign can be attributed to many factors. The new Chinese attitude, which favored suppression of the drug, was the primary reason the campaign enjoyed the success that it did. But the foreign opium merchants, who had sold the drug for a century, were also responsible for helping to suppress

it when they finally asked the British government to stop
selling opium in India, since there was no market for it in
China. And the change of opinion among British political
leaders allowed them to alter their policies on opium just
as the Chinese were demanding that those changes be made.
If the missionaries were not directly responsible for the
eradication of opium from China in the early 1900s it mat-
tered not at all to them, since the goal they had sought for
so long was finally in sight and they could glory in that accomplishment.

Appendix

Questions asked in the survey of Western-trained medical doctors in China (see chapter 2) and published as William H. Park, M.D., comp., *Opinions of Over 100 Physicians on the Use of Opium in China* (Shanghai: American Presbyterian Mission Press, 1899).

1. What have you observed to be the effects of opium, moral, physical and social, on its consumers?
2. What are the proportions of those who smoke opium:
    A. Without injury?
    B. With slight injury?
    C. With great injury ("opium sots")?
3. A. Is the number of opium-smokers increasing in your district?
    B. Do women smoke to any extent?
    C. Do children smoke?
    D. Do the effects of opium-smoking by parents show in their children?
4. Is there a tendency to increase amount smoked?
5. Can a person, in your opinion, smoke opium daily for years without becoming a confirmed opium smoker?
6. A. What percentage of laborers, merchants, and artisans smoke opium in the part of China with which you are acquainted?
    B. What is the effect of opium on their efficiency?
    C. Do many employers object to employing opium smokers?
    D. If so, what are some of the reasons assigned for not employing them?
7. Is the opium habit condemned as degrading or injurious by the Chinese in general?

8. How do they regard the opium habit as compared with the alcohol habit?

9. Is opium, within your knowledge, a prophylactic against fever, rheumatism, or malaria?

10. Is it so regarded commonly by the inhabitants of the part of China with which you are conversant?

11. A. Do Chinese physicians prescribe opium smoking for chronic illnesses?
    B. If so, and relief is afforded, is it temporary or permanent?

12. A. Is suicide common in your section of China?
    B. What is the agent most generally employed?

13. A. Do opium smokers usually desire to get free of the habit?
    B. Can they break themselves of it?
    C. Are opium-cure morphia pills freely sold in your city?

14. If you run an opium refuge, do you cut off opium suddenly or gradually?

15. If opium is cut off suddenly do the patients suffer? If so, give symptoms.

16. A. Give percentage of smokers who began for some ailment.
    B. Give percentage of your permanent cures of the opium habit.
    C. What number, after being cured, have joined the Church.

17. Can you give any estimate of the area under cultivation of the poppy in your part of China, and the average out-turn of opium?

18. Have you any other remarks to make in regard to opium smoking among the Chinese?

Notes

Abbreviations

Chinese Recorder	*CR*
Friend of China	*FC*
International Opium Commission	IOC
North China Herald	*NCH*

Introduction

1. Sizes of chests were not uniform. Malwa opium was shipped in 135-pound chests while the Bengal variety arrived in 160-pound chests. Morse, *Trade and Administration*, Chapter 9 deals with opium; see particularly 337-38 for statistics.

2. Ibid., 351. A picul equals 133 ⅓ English pounds, so was roughly equivalent to the chests in which the earlier trade had been measured.

3. Ibid., 337-38, 351, 360.

4. For a discussion of the opium trade between legalization and the renegotiation of the opium duties in 1883 see Waung, *Controversy*. Waung focuses primarily on the impact the opium trade had upon Hong Kong and the issues involved in the 1883 renegotiations of the likin rates, which were not collected until 1887. Although he makes several references to the Anglo-Oriental Society for the Suppression of the Opium Trade, he fails to explore it as a pressure group and only briefly links it to missionaries in China and at home. His work contains a number of useful appendices on the statistics of the opium trade, particularly with regard to Hong Kong.

5. Royal Commission on Opium, *Final Report*, 6:141.

6. Courtwright, *Dark Paradise*, 54-56.

7. For an account of the opium problem as an issue in the foreign policy of the Western countries in the twentieth century see Walker, *Opium and Foreign Policy*.

8. M.C. Wright, *China in Revolution*, 14.

9. H. Wright, "Report on the Opium Conference at Shanghai," 94.

1. OPIUM IN CHINA IN THE LATE NINETEENTH CENTURY

1. Scott, *The White Poppy*, 1.

2. Merlin, *On the Trail of the Ancient Opium Poppy*, 147-78. Chapter 6 of this work, "Possible Places of Cultural Origin for the Opium Poppy," is a discussion of the latest archaeological finds.

3. Morse, *International Relations*, 1:172-73.

4. Morse, *Trade and Administration*, 348, 350-51, 353.

5. Fairbank, Bruner, and Matheson, *I.G. in Peking*, letter no. 142, n 3.

6. Scott, *White Poppy*, 2-3. Scott also gives a brief history of the poppy plant.

7. China, *Opium*, 69.

8. Ibid., 73-74.

9. Ibid., 13, 45.

10. Ibid., 21-22.

11. China, *Native Opium*, 3-52, chart facing 52.

12. Ibid., 3-19, 28-29.

13. Ibid., 46.

14. Ibid., 39-40.

15. Ibid., 14, 20, 26, 45, chart facing 52.

16. Ibid., 3-52, chart facing 52.

17. Ibid.

18. Ibid.

19. Hart estimated each chest of imported opium weighed 100 catties. There were 16 liang in a catty and ten mace in a liang. He used the average of three mace for each pipe smoked and placed the population of China at 300 million but noted that some thought it might be closer to 400 million. China, *Opium*, 1-4.

20. Ibid., 51.

21. Ibid., 55.

22. China, *Native Opium*, 6, 14.

23. Robertson-Scott, *People of China*, 141.

24. Bard, *Chinese Life in Town and Country*, 159-60.

25. Gamewell, "From Shanghai into Western China," 36.

26. Ball, *Things Chinese*, 434.

27. Spence, "Opium Smoking in Ch'ing China," 154.

28. James Mackey of the Customs office in Wenchow was one of the many Westerners in China who reported that addicts first used opium to alleviate pain or cure an illness. See China, *Opium*, 36.

29. Pruitt, *Daughter of Han*, 46. Pruitt's account covers the years 1867-1938.

30. "The Friend of China: A Review of the October 1890 Issue," *CR* 21 (Jan. 1891), 38. See also, *FC* 9 (Oct. 1890), 304.

31. Francis W. White, commissioner of Customs at Hankow, was one of the many Westerners who linked the lack of a "robust constitution" of the addict to the effects of addiction. See China, *Opium*, 19.

32. Gamewell, "From Shanghai into Western China," 36.

33. Spence, "Opium Smoking in Ch'ing China," 144.

34. The missionary was Maud Killam, M.D., of the Canadian Methodist Mission, who reported the incident in *Missionary Outlook*, Aug. 1899, 191, cited in Gagan, *Sensitive Independence*, 137.

35. Moule, *New China and Old*, 185.

36. Chang Hsin-pao, *Commissioner Lin*, 131, 134.

37. China, *Opium*, 13-14, 19.

2. MISSIONARIES ORGANIZE TO OPPOSE OPIUM

1. "Chinese Statement on the Opium Traffic," *FC* 14 (July 1893), 137-41. See also Teng and Fairbank, *China's Response to the West*, 24.

2. Broomhall, *Truth About Opium Smoking*, 76-77. See also J. G. Alexander, "Mr. Alexander's Interviews with Chinese Statesmen," *FC* 15 (Dec. 1894), 97-98.

3. Cleife, *England's Greatest National Sin*, 75.

4. Johnston, *Report of the Centenary Conference*, 1:129.

5. For a general discussion of the early work of missionaries in the anti-opium movement see Beattie, "Protestant Missions and Opium in China," 104-33.

6. "Editorial," *CR* 1 (Jan. 1868), 93-95.

7. "Historical Summary of the *Chinese Recorder*," *CR* 46 (July 1914), 446-49.

8. "Editorial," *CR* 22 (Aug. 1891), 391.

9. "Editorial," *CR* 23 (Nov. 1892), 541.

10. "Editorial," *CR* 25 (Jan. 1894), 47.

11. William Muirhead, "Appeal to the Missionaries in China on the Opium Question," *FC* 18 (Oct. 1898), 94-98.

12. Latourette, *History of Christian Missions*, 457-58.

13. Prince Kung was reported to have told Sir Rutherford Alcock in 1869, "Take away your opium and your missionaries, and you will be welcome." See Morse, *International Relations*, 2:220.

14. "Farewell to Archdeacon Moule," *FC* 23 (Jan. 1903), 8. This question was posed to many missionaries who sought to preach Christianity to the Chinese. See Cleife, *England's Greatest National Sin*, 37, for the bishop of Victoria's experience with the question and 66 for the Rev. J. Hudson Taylor's experience.

15. "Editorial," *CR* 23 (Nov. 1892), 540.

16. "Editorial," *CR* 24 (Dec. 1893), 595-96.

17. "Notes and Items," *CR* 26 (July 1895), 330-31.

18. "Notes and Items," *CR* 26 (Oct. 1895), 479.

19. "Notes and Items," *CR* 27 (Mar. 1896), 142-43. The Rev. Justus Doolittle had written one of the earliest of the missionary tracts against opium in 1853, which he published in the Foochow colloquial, following it two years later with a literary version, see Barnett, "Justus Doolittle at Foochow," 114-15.

20. "Anglo-Oriental" was quickly dropped from the society's name. For a discussion of the social context in which the Society was organized, see Berridge and Edwards, *Opium and the People*, 173-94.

21. "Missionary Conference," *NCH* 16 May 1890, 602-3.

22. Ibid.

23. Ibid., 658. Denominational affiliations of missionaries here and following are from Lodwick, *The CHINESE RECORDER Index*, vol. 1.

24. J.G. Kerr and Grainger Hargreaves, "The Opium Question: Report of the Committee on the Opium Traffic," *CR* 22 (Aug. 1891), 371-72. See also "Notes and Extracts," *FC* 13 (Jan. 1892), 39-40.

25. "Editorial," *CR* 22 (Aug. 1891), 391.

26. "Shansi Conference of Protestant Missionaries, September 29 to October 5, 1892," *CR* 24 (Apr. 1893), 186.

27. "Editorial," *CR* 24 (May 1893), 244.

28. "Missionary News: The Anti-Opium League," *CR* 27 (June 1896), 308-9.

29. "Missionary News: National Anti-Opium League," *CR* 28 (May 1897), 246.

30. "Missionary News: Anti-Opium League," *CR* 29 (June 1898), 307.

31. Park, *Opinions of Over 100 Physicians*, iv.

32. Ibid., 1, 2, 3, 8.

33. Ibid., 9-12.

34. Ibid., 13.

35. Ibid., 15-16.

36. Ibid., 25-26.

37. Ibid., 29-32.

38. Ibid., 32-33.

39. Ibid., 34-40.

40. Ibid., 42-43.

41. Gamewell, "From Shanghai into Western China," 36. The suicides reported by CIM missionaries in Chungking are also mentioned in Parker, *John Chinaman*, 20.

42. Park, *Opinions of Over 100 Physicians*, 34-43. One author stated the rescue of a person attempting suicide by swallowing opium was the most common medical story reported by doctors in China. See Austin, *Saving China*, 173-74.

43. Park, *Opinions of Over 100 Physicians*, 57.

44. Ibid., 62-63, 65.

45. Ibid., 62. For articles using Park's study as a source see T.G. Selby, "The Opinions of Over 100 Physicians on the Use of Opium in China," *FC* 20 (Jan. 1900), 3-6; and Cornaby, "Opium in China," 93 (Jan. 1900), 131-39.

46. Hampden C. DuBose, "Letter to the Editor," *CR* 29 (Apr. 1898), 190.

47. "Missionary Notes: The Anti-Opium League in China," *CR* 29 (Nov. 1898), 565.

48. "Missionary News: Anti-Opium League in China," *CR* 30 (Jan. 1899), 50-51.

49. "Missionary News: Anti-Opium League in China," *CR* 30 (Aug. 1899), 412-13.

50. "Missionary News: Anti-Opium League Notes," *CR* 31 (Mar. 1900), 156.

51. Johnston, *Report of the Centenary Conference*, 1:131.

52. Ibid., 133-34.

53. Ibid., 471.

54. Ibid., 475.

55. Hood, "Introductory Study," 90.

56. "Missionary News: The Society of Friends on the Opium Traffic with China," *CR* 31 (Oct. 1901), 527.

57. "Summary," *FC* 15 (Oct. 1895), 191.

58. "Editorial," *CR* 23 (Jan. 1892), 43.

59. Quoted in "Editorial," *CR* 23 (Nov. 1892), 541.

60. Although different Chinese characters, Yen's name is spelled in English the same way as the character for the craving for opium.

61. "Farewell Meetings to Mr. Yen," *FC* 15 (Oct. 1894), 62.

62. Ibid.

63. "Death of Rev. Yung King Yen," *FC* 18 (Oct. 1898), 82.

64. Moule's brothers, George Evans Moule, bishop of mid-China, and the Rev. D. Handley Moule, bishop of Durham, England, and his son, Walter, also an archdeacon, were all active in the anti-opium movement.

65. "Archdeacon Moule on China and Opium," *FC* 13 (Mar. 1892), 66.

66. "Farewell to Archdeacon Moule," *FC* 23 (Jan. 1903), 10-11.

67. Ibid., 13-14.

68. Harding, *Opiate Addiction*, 26, and Brown, "Politics of the Poppy," 100-101.

69. Harding, *Opiate Addiction*, 26. Another member of the Matheson family, Hugh, in 1834 refused to join the firm because of its involvement in the opium trade. See also Hood, "Introductory Study," 89-90.

70. Harding, *Opiate Addiction*, 26.

71. See Lim, "Britain and the Termination," 26.

72. "Statement of Facts and Principles Upon Which the Action of the Society for the Suppression of the Opium Trade is Based," *FC* 9 (Mar. 1886), 5.

73. For a discussion of the political manuevering that took place in Parliament when the subject came up and at the time of the appointment of the royal commission see Owen, *British Opium Policy*, 312-28.

74. "Debate on Sir Joseph Pease's Motion," *FC* 12 (May 1891), 86-87.

75. Quoted in Archbishop Moule, "Speech at the Annual Meeting of the Society," *FC* 12 (July 1891), 199.

76. Cleife, *England's Greatest National Sin*, iv.

77. J.G. Alexander, "Mr. Alexander's Report to the Committee," *FC* 15 (Dec. 1894), 91.

78. J.G. Alexander, "Mr. Alexander's Interviews with Chinese Statesmen," *FC* 15 (Dec. 1894), 95.

79. Chang Chih-tung, *Learn*. Also see Chang Chih-tung, *China's Only Hope*, 72-77.

80. J.G. Alexander, "Letter to the Editor," *CR* 30 (July 1894), 350-51. Alexander said, "This plan was based on hints thrown out originally by Chinese statesmen." See J.G. Alexander, "Mr Alexander's Report," *FC* 15 (Dec. 1894), 94. The origin of the plan is uncertain. Beattie attributes it to an unidentified Indian civil servant. Archdeacon Moule proposed it at the 1877 missionary conference in

London. Chang Chih-tung mentioned it in an interview in 1883.

81. J.G. Alexander, "Mr. Alexander's Interviews," 96-98.

82. J.G. Alexander, "Letter to the Editor," *CR* 30 (July 1894), 350-51.

83. J.G. Alexander, "Mr. Alexander's Report," 90.

84. J.G. Alexander, "Mr. Alexander's Interviews," 93, 99.

85. J.G. Alexander, "Mr. Alexander's Report," 93.

86. "Reminder to Missionaries Going on Furlough," *FC* 17 (Oct. 1897), 102.

87. "Annual Meeting of the Society," *FC* 20 (July 1900), 41-42.

88. "Summary," *FC* 20 (Oct. 1900), 49.

89. George Hudson, "The Causes of the Outbreak in China," *FC* 20 (July 1900), 38.

90. "Summary," *FC* 20 (Oct. 1900), 51-53. See also Esherick, *Origins of the Boxer Uprising*, 19-21.

91. "Representative Board's Manifesto," *FC* 20 (Oct. 1900), 53-55.

92. "A Weighty Memorial," *FC* 22 (Apr. 1902), 26-27.

93. "Christian Anti-Opium Convention," *FC* 12 (May 1891), 103-8.

94. "Summary," *FC* 13 (July 1892), 111-12. A two-hour prayer meeting also preceded the 1894 annual meeting. See "Annual Meeting," *FC* 15 (Dec. 1894), 99.

95. "Reminder to Missionaries Going on Furlough," *FC* 17 (Oct. 1897), 102.

96. Quoted in "Renewed Opposition to the Opium Traffic: Deputation from India," *CR* 21 (Mar. 1890), 138.

97. "Missionary Notes," *CR* 24 (Feb. 1893), 97.

98. MacGillivray, *Century of Protestant Missions*, 172.

99. "Notes and Extracts," *FC* 12 (Mar. 1891), 74.

100. "Editorial," *CR* 30 (July 1899), 357.

101. "Opium Drain of Silver from South China," *NCH*, 28 Mar. 1890, 365.

102. "Opium Drain of Silver," *NCH*, 21 Mar. 1890, 334.

103. "The Blackburn Commercial Mission to China," *FC* 18 (Oct. 1898), 92-93.

3. THE PRO-OPIUM FORCES AND GOVERNMENT INVESTIGATIONS

1. Rees, *India*, 130.

2. The 1892-93 figures are estimates. The sum of the Bengal duties and the transit taxes do not equal the total revenue. "Extract from a Speech of Sir Joseph Pease," *CR* 24 (Oct. 1893), 479.

3. R. Brown, *Opium Revenue and Indian Finance*, 3.

4. "Editorial," *CR* 24 (Feb. 1893), 93.

5. "Editorial," *CR* 41 (Dec. 1910), 701.

6 "Editorial," *CR* 24 (Feb. 1893), 94.

7. R. Brown, *Opium Revenue and Indian Finance*, 22.

8. The origins of the Sassoon family are not clear. Although some scholars think they were Sephardic in origin, others attribute their roots to the Middle East as they had long served the rulers of Baghdad as financial managers. See Roth, *Sassoon Dynasty*, 21.

9. Hyde, *Far Eastern Trade*, 53.

10. Charles, "Olyphant and Opium," 67, and Hoe, *Private Life*, 17.

11. Batten, "Opium Question," 454, 456, 467.

12. Ibid., 453.

13. Ibid., 474-75.

14. Ibid., 456-57.

15. Ibid. 463.

16. Ibid., 471.

17. Ibid., 473-74.

18. Ibid., 477, 478, 484.

19. Ibid., 484-85. Another speaker at the meeting, Sir Joseph Fayrer, who had spent many years in India, said, "There is another drug which is also in frequent use in India, the hemp (*cannabis*), which is infinitely worse than opium. I find no objection taken to this drug by the anti-opium party," 483.

20. Ibid., 485.

21. Ibid., 487-88.

22. Ibid., 494.

23. Montagu Beauchamp, "Some Pro-Opium Arguments Dissected," *FC* 22 (Apr. 1902), 20.

24. Ibid., 21-23, 25.

25. Reid, "Behar Planter," 42-43.

26. Sultzberger, *All About Opium*, 118-19.

27. Kane, *Opium-Smoking in America and China*, 75.

28. Brereton, *Truth About Opium*, 88.

29. Moore, *Other Side of the Opium Question*, 59.

30. Barker, "India and the Opium Traffic," 47-48.

31. Rowntree, *Opium Habit*, 4-5. See also H. Alexander, *Joseph Gundry Alexander*, 63-64.

32. "Editorial," *CR* 24 (Oct. 1893), 493-94.

33. Rowntree, *Opium Habit*, 4-5.

34. "Constitution of the Royal Commission," *FC* 15 (Dec. 1894), 72-73. W.S. Caine, a member of the Society for the Suppression of

the Opium Trade and a leader of the anti-opium group in Parliament, was appointed to serve on the commission but was unable to carry out his duties and was replaced at the fourth meeting by Henry J. Wilson, who was an opponent of the opium trade even though he had not been active in the anti-opium movement. See H. Alexander, *Joseph Gundry Alexander*, 64-65.

35. "Editorial," *CR* 24 (Oct. 1893), 494.
36. J. G. Alexander, "Mr. Alexander's Interviews," 96-97.
37. "Constitution of the Royal Commission," *FC* 15 (Dec. 1894), 72-73.
38. Kitson Clark, *Critical Historian*, 78-79.
39. "Important Joint Statement and Appeal: The Royal Commission on Opium," *FC* 14 (Jan. 1894), 180.
40. Ibid., 181-83.
41. "Editorial," *CR* 25 (Jan. 1894), 46-47.
42. H. Alexander, *Joseph Gundry Alexander*, 68.
43. Rowntree, *Opium Habit*, 88-90.
44. Ibid. One author termed Brenan "one of the most qualified British consuls in China." See Pelcovits, *Old China Hands*, 195.
45. Rowntree, *Opium Habit*, 86.
46. Ibid., 90-91.
47. The questions of the Royal Commission were essentially the same as those used by William H. Park several years later in compiling *Opinions of Over 100 Physicians*.
48. Griffith John, "The Rev. Griffith John, On Opium in China," *CR* 25 (Apr. 1894), 198.
49. De Voeux, "Letter to the Opium Commission," 324.
50. Ibid., 328.
51. John, "Rev. Griffith John," 198-99.
52. Ibid., 200.
53. Ibid.
54. "Editorial," *CR* 25 (Jan. 1894), 47.
55. "Letter to Editor," *CR* 25 (Feb. 1894), 138.
56. "Missionary News: Copy of Memorial Presented to the Royal Commission on Opium by Missionaries in China of Twenty-five or More Years Service," *CR* 25 (June 1894), 308.
57. Royal Commission on Opium, *Final Report*, 6:50-51.
58. Ibid., 61.
59. Rowntree, *Opium Habit*, 1.
60. Ibid., 103-4, 108.
61. Ibid., 53-54.

62. "Editorial," *CR* 24 (Sept. 1893), 443.

63. Rowntree, *Opium Habit*, 84.

64. Ibid., 84-86.

65. Foster, *Report of the Royal Commission*, iii-ix.

66. Ibid., 1-2.

67. Ibid., 16.

68. Ibid., 2.

69. Ibid., 6.

70. Ibid., 7-8.

71. Ibid., 6-10, 40-41.

72. Ibid., 13.

73. Ibid., 11-12.

74. Ibid., 14-15, 17.

75. Ibid., 19.

76. Ibid., 21, 22.

77. Ibid., 25.

78. Ibid., 26-29.

79. Ibid.

80. Ibid., 33.

81. Ibid., 31-34.

82. Ibid., 39.

83. Zabriskie, *Bishop Brent*, 98.

84. U. S., War Department, Bureau of Insular Affairs, *Report*, 51.

85. Ibid., 3-4.

86. Ibid., 77-84.

87. Ibid., 75-76.

88. Ibid., 87-89.

89. Ibid., 45-47.

90. Ibid., 47-48.

91. Ibid., 20-21.

92. Ibid., 21.

93. Ibid., 20-23.

94. Ibid., 26.

95. Ibid., 27.

4. The Anti-Opium Lobby Comes of Age

1. Cameron, *Reform Movement in China*, 136. See also, M. Wright, *China in Revolution*, 14-15.

2. IOC. *Report*, 2:78. See also Yu, *Chung-kuo chin yen fa-ling pien-ch'ien shih*, 261; and Shen, *Kuang Hsu Cheng-yao*, 2319.

3. IOC, *Report*, 2:79.
4. Ibid., 82.
5. Ibid., 79.
6. Ibid., 92.
7. Ibid., 105-6.
8. Lim, "Britain and Termination," 49.
9. H. Alexander, *Joseph Gundry Alexander*, 130; Lim, "Britain and Termination," 65, 67.
10. Lim, "Britain and Termination," 65.
11. H. Alexander, *Joseph Gundry Alexander*, 130.
12. Lim, "Britain and Termination," 78-79.
13. Yu, *Chung-kuo chin yen fa-ling pein-ch'ien shih*, 120-21.
14. Foreign Office, *Opium Trade*, vol. 1, part 1, 25.
15. Anti-Opium League, *Greater Year of Anti-Opium*, 16.
16. Ibid.
17. IOC, *Report*, 2:117.
18. Anti-Opium League, *Greater Year of Anti-Opium*, 15.
19. Ibid., 14.
20. Ibid., 1. See Yu, *Chung-kuo chin yen fa-ling pien-ch'ien shih*, 263, for the Chinese version.
21. Anti-Opium League, *Greater Year of Anti-Opium*, 1.
22. Ibid., 2.
23. Ibid., 16.
24. Ibid.
25. China Centenary Missionary Conference, *Records*, 389-90.
26. Ibid., 649.
27. Ibid., 646-48.
28. American Board of Commissioners for Foreign Missions, *Annual Report*, 156.
29. Park, *Opinions of Over 100 Physicians*, 49.
30. De Gruche, *Doctor Apricot*, 29-30.
31. Moir Duncan, "English Baptist Mission, Shensi: Second Annual Report, Year Ending December 1893," *CR* 25 (July 1894), 319-20.
32. Latourette, *History of Christian Missions*, 457.
33. Park, *Opinions of Over 100 Physicians*, 46, 47. Yao and Shun are the sage rulers of Chinese antiquity.
34. "Eleventh Annual Report of the Williams Hospital at Pan Chuang, Shantung for 1890," *CR* 23 (Jan. 1892), 38.
35. Towns, *Habits that Handicap*, 37.
36. George L. Mason, "Morphine Habit Spreading," *CR* 24 (July 1893), 350.

37. Conference Internationale de L'Opium, *Actes et Documents*, 78-83.

38. G. King, "Cure of Opium Smokers," *CR* 21 (Oct. 1890), 458-61.

39. John Dudgeon, "Letter to the Editor," *CR* 21 (Nov. 1890), 517.

40. "Opium Cure," *Chinese Medical Missionary Journal* 4 (Dec. 1890): 249.

41. Dudgeon, "Letter to the Editor," 517.

42. Latourette, *History of Christian Missions*, 457.

43. IOC, *Report*, 1:3-7.

44. Ibid., 9-10.

45. Ibid., 15.

46. Ibid., 21.

47. Ibid., 29-30.

48. Ibid., 29, 30, 32.

49. Ibid., 38.

50. Ibid., 54.

51. Ibid., 65-67, 70.

52. Ibid., 84.

53. Commons, *Sessional Papers*, Cd. 6038, miscellaneous no. 2, 11-16.

54. Willoughby, *Opium as an International Problem*, 26-27.

55. Ibid., 30-32.

56. Ibid., 35-36.

57. IOC, *Report*, 1:67. Opium revenues were being used to finance China's armaments business. See Kennedy, "Mausers and the Opium Trade," 119.

58. IOC, *Report*, 1:67-68.

59. "Summary," *FC* 26 (Apr. 1909), 27.

60. "Editorial," *CR* 40 (Oct. 1909), 541.

61. Sargent, *Anglo-Chinese Commerce*, 267-68.

62. Remer, *Foreign Trade of China*, 157.

5. SUCCESS AND FAILURES OF OPIUM SUPPRESSION

1. For a discussion of the parliamentary debate on this aspect of the opium question, see Wu, *Chinese Opium Question*, 160-65.

2. IOC, *Report*, 2:117, 356.

3. Ibid., 57-58.

4. Hosie, *On the Trail of the Opium Poppy*, 1:2. For Hosie's report

on Shansi, Shensi, and Kansu see Foreign Office, *Opium Trade*, vol. 1, part 2, 137-54.

5. Hosie, *On the Trail of the Opium Poppy*, 1:4; 2:233.

6. Ibid., 2:236, 238-39.

7. Ibid., 1:5.

8. Ibid., 1:5, 41-42, 43, 51, 53, 57, 58-59.

9. Ibid., 1:66; 2:241.

10. Ibid., 1:67.

11. Ibid., 73-74.

12. Ibid., 2:242-43.

13. Ibid., 244, 246-47.

14. Ibid., 250.

15. Ibid., 1:123.

16. Ibid., 2:250, 256.

17. Ibid., 1:130; 2:250.

18. Ibid., 1:127-28.

19. Ibid., 213, 214.

20. Ibid., 241, 242-43, 260-61, 266; 2:6, 21. For Hosie's report on Szechwan, see Foreign Office, *Opium Trade*, vol. 1, part 3, 97-100.

21. Hosie, *On The Trail of the Opium Poppy*, 2:58, 59, 64, 65, 75, 76, 84.

22. Ibid., 275, 276-77. For Hosie's report on Yunnan, see Foreign Office, *Opium Trade*, vol. 1, part 3, 142-44.

23. Hosie, *On The Trail of the Opium Poppy*, 2:117-18.

24. Ibid., 102, 110, 112.

25. Ibid., 128-29.

26. Ibid., 165, 279, 280-81, 287. For Hosie's report on Kweichow, see Foreign Office, *Opium Trade*, vol. 1, part 3, 193-96.

27. Hosie, *On the Trail of the Opium Poppy*, 2:287-88.

28. Chung-kuo K'o-hsueh-yuan, *Hsi-liang i-kao tsou-kao*, 650.

29. Foreign Office, *Opium Trade*, vol. 1, part 3, 167.

30. Adshead, "Opium Trade in Szechwan," 96.

31. Parliamentary Papers, *China No. 3*, 47.

32. Adshead, "Opium Trade in Szechwan," 98, 99.

33. Parliamentary Papers, *Report of the British Delegates*, 6.

34. Des Forges, *Hsi-liang*, 96.

35. Hedley, *Tramps in Dark Mongolia*, 45.

36. Wilder, "China's Attack on the Opium Problem," 221.

37. "Progress of the Anti-Opium Movement Among the Chinese," *CR* 29 (Mar. 1908), 143, 145, 146-47.

38. Ibid., 148-50.

39. Ibid., 153.

40. Foreign Office, *Opium Trade*, vol. 1, part 3, 167.

41. Ibid., 104-8.

42. Ibid., 169-70.

43. Ibid., part 4, 63. See also 73-75, 84-86.

44. Documentation of the Sassoons' complaints is extensive. See Ibid., vol. 1, part 2, 73-74; part 2, 14-16, 50, 79, 98-99, 105; part 3, 33, 68, 134, 141, 191-92; part 4, 4, 16, 23-24, 33; vol. 2, part 5, 55-56, 134-35, 138-39, 142, 164, 174.

45. Ibid., vol. 2, part 6, 58. For Jordan's report see 80-81.

46. Ibid., 60, 66, 67, 68-69.

47. Ibid., 102, 103-4, 123-25. For Fraser's complete report, see 100-10.

48. Ibid., vol. 1, part 3, 127.

49. Ibid., 126.

50. Ibid., vol. 2, part 5, 129.

51. Ibid., 130. Taylor's statement was made at the 1888 Centenary Conference of the Protestant Missions of the World held in London and is quoted in Crafts, *Intoxicants and Opium*, 108.

52. Foreign Office, *Opium Trade*, vol. 2, part 5, 66-67; part 6, 9.

53. Ibid., vol. 2, part 6, 40-41; vol. 3, part 7, 26-27.

54. Ibid., vol. 2, part 5, 59; vol. 3, part 7, 55-56.

55. Ibid., vol. 2, part 5, 61; for the complete statements of Yuan and Sun, see vol. 2, part 5, 71-74.

56. Ibid., vol. 2, part 6, 153.

57. Ibid., 26-27.

58. Ibid., 13-14.

59. Ibid., vol. 3, part 7, 29-30, 34.

60. Ibid., part 8, 7.

61. Ibid., 8.

62. Lim, "Britain and Termination," 376. See also 357-77 for a detailed discussion of the view of British government officials on the question of the opium stocks and their attitude toward Jordan's suggestions for solving the problem.

63. Foreign Office, *Opium Trade*, vol. 3, part 9, 30-31; part 10, 17.

64. Harding, *Opiate Addiction*, 29-30.

Bibliography

Adshead, S.A.M. "Opium Trade in Szechwan, 1881-1911." *Journal of Southeast Asian History* 7 (Sept. 1966): 93-99.

Alexander, Horace G. *Joseph Gundry Alexander.* London: Swarthmore Press, 1921.

American Board of Commissioners for Foreign Missions. *Annual Report, 1906.* Boston: American Board Publishing Department, 1906.

Anti-Opium League. *Greater Year of Anti-Opium: The Annual Report of the Anti-Opium League.* Shanghai: North-China Daily News and Herald, 1909.

Austin, Alvyn J. *Saving China: Canadian Missionaries in the Middle Kingdom, 1888-1959.* Toronto: University of Toronto Press, 1986.

Ball, J. Dyer. *Things Chinese or Notes Connected with China.* Shanghai: Kelly and Walsh, 1925.

Bard, Emile. *Chinese Life in Town and Country.* Trans. from the French by H. Twitchell. London: G.P. Putnam's Sons, 1907.

Barker, D.A. "India and the Opium Traffic." *Economic Review* 20 (Jan. 1910): 41-50.

Barnett, Suzanne Wilson. "Justus Doolittle at Foochow: Christian Values in the Treaty Ports." In *Christianity in China: Early Protestant Missionary Writing,* ed. Suzanne Wilson Barnett and John King Fairbank. Cambridge: Council on East Asian Studies, Harvard University, 1985.

Batten, G.H.M. "The Opium Question." *Journal of the [Royal] Society of Arts* 40 (Apr. 1, 1892): 444-94.

Beattie, Hillary J. "Protestant Missions and Opium in China, 1858-1895." *Harvard Papers on China* 22A (May 1969): 104-33.

Berridge, Virginia, and Griffith Edwards. *Opium and the People: Opiate Use in Nineteenth-Century England.* London: Allen Lane, 1981.

Brereton, William H. *The Truth About Opium: Being a Refutation of* the Fallacies of the Anti-opium Society and a Defence of the Indo-China Opium Trade. London: W.H. Allen, 1883.

Broomhall, Benjamin. The Chinese Opium Smoker. London [?]: Society for the Suppression of the Opium Trade [?], n.d.

——. Truth About Opium Smoking. London: Hodder and Stoughton, 1882.

——. The Evangelization of the World: A Missionary Band, A Record of Consecration and an Appeal. London: Morgan and Scott, 1886.

Brown, Arthur J. New Forces in Old China: An Unwelcome But Inevitable Awakening. New York: F.H. Revell, 1904.

Brown, James B. "Politics of the Poppy: The Society for the Suppression of the Opium Trade, 1874-1916." Journal of Contemporary History 8 (July 1973): 97-111.

Brown, Robert. The Opium Revenue and Indian Finance. Glasgow: Charles Glass, 1891 [?].

Cameron, Meribeth. Reform Movement in China 1898-1912. Stanford: Stanford University Press, 1931.

Chang Chih-tung. China's Only Hope: An Appeal by her Greatest Viceroy, Chang Chih-tung. Trans. Samuel I. Woodbridge. New York: F.H. Revell, 1900.

Chang Chih-tung. Learn. Taipei: Wen Hai, 1967.

Chang Hsin-pao. Commissioner Lin and the Opium War. New York: W.W. Norton, 1964.

Charles, Robert. "Olyphant and Opium: A Canton Merchant Who 'Just Said "No"'." International Bulletin of Missionary Research 16 (April 1992): 66-69.

China. Inspectorate General of Customs. Imperial Maritime Customs, II, Special Series, no. 9. Native Opium, 1887, With An Appendix: Native Opium, 1863. Shanghai: Statistical Department of the Inspectorate General of Customs, 1888.

——. Special Series, no. 4. Opium. Shanghai: Inspector General of Customs, 1881.

China Centenary Missionary Conference, Shanghai, 1907. Records of the China Centenary Missionary Conference held at Shanghai, April 25 to May 8, 1907. Shanghai: Centenary Conference Committee, 1907.

Chinese Recorder. 1 (Jan. 1868)—48 (Dec. 1917).

Chung-kuo K'o-hsueh-yuan. [Chinese Academy of Science (Academica Sinica)]. Comp. Hsi-liang i-kao tsou-kao [Memorials of

Hsi-liang, Published Posthumously]. Taipei: China Publishing, 1959.

Cleife, Henry H.T. *England's Greatest National Sin: Being Selections and Reflections on our Asiatic Opium Policy and Traffic.* London: Elliot Stock, 1892.

Conference Internationale de L'Opium, La Haye, 1 Dec. 1911-23 Jan. 1912. *Actes et Documents.* La Haye: Ministere des Affaires Etrangeres, 1912.

Cornaby, W. Arthur. "Opium in China." *London Quarterly Review* 93 (Jan. 1900): 131-39.

Courtwright, David T. *Dark Paradise: Opiate Addiction in America before 1940.* Cambridge: Harvard University Press, 1982.

Crafts, Wilbur F., et. al. *Intoxicants and Opium in All Lands and Times: A Twentieth-Century Survey of Intemperance, Based on a Symposium of Testimony from One Hundred Missionaries and Travelers.* Washington: International Reform Bureau, 1900.

De Gruche, Kingston. *Doctor Apricot of "Heaven Below": The Story of the Hangchow Medical Mission (C.M.S.).* London: Marshall, 1911.

Des Forges, Roger V. *Hsi-liang and the Chinese National Revolution.* New Haven: Yale University Press, 1973.

De Voeux, G.W. "Letter to the Opium Commission." *Nineteenth Century* 35 (1894): 323-29.

Esherick, Joseph. *The Origins of the Boxer Uprising.* Berkeley: University of California Press, 1987.

Fairbank, John King. *Trade and Diplomacy on the China Coast: The Opening of the Treaty Ports, 1842-1854.* Cambridge: Harvard University Press, 1953.

Fairbank, John King, Katherine Frost Bruner, and Elizabeth MacLeod Matheson, eds. *The I.G. in Peking: Letters of Robert Hart, Chinese Maritime Customs 1868-1907.* 2 vols. Cambridge: Belknap Press of Harvard University Press, 1975.

Foster, Arnold. *Report of the Royal Commission on Opium Compared with the Evidence from China that was Submitted to the Commission: An Examination and An Appeal.* London: Eyre and Spottiswoode, 1899.

Friend of China. 9 (Mar. 1886)—26 (Apr. 1909).

Gagan, Rosemary R. *A Sensitive Independence: Canadian Methodist Women Missionaries in Canada and the Orient, 1881-1925.* Montreal: McGill-Queen's University Press, 1992.

Gamewell, F.D. "From Shanghai into Western China." *Gospel in All Lands* 14 (Jan. 1888): 33-37.

Great Britain. Foreign Office. *Opium Trade, 1910-1940.* Facsimile reproduction of the Foreign Office Collection (F.O. 415) in the Public Record Office, London. 6 vols. Wilmington, Del.: Scholarly Resources, 1974.

———. House of Commons. *Sessional Papers, 1912-13. International Opium Convention.* Cd. 6038, miscellaneous no. 2, (1912).

———. Parliamentary Papers. *China No. 3 (1909). Despatches from His Majesty's Minister at Peking, Forwarding Reports Respecting the Opium Question in China.* Cd. 4967, 13 (1910).

———. Parliamentary Papers. Misc. no. 11 (1912). *Report of the British Delegates to the International Opium Conference held at The Hague, December 1911-January 1912.* Cd. 6448. London: Harrison and Sons, 1912.

———. Royal Commission on Opium. 7 vols. Vol. 1, *First Report of the Royal Commission on Opium with Minutes of Evidence and Appendices.* Vol. 2, 3, 4, *Minutes of Evidence Taken Before the Royal Commission on Opium from 29 Jan. to 22 Feb. 1894 with Appendices.* Vol. 5, *Appendices Together with Correspondence on the Subject of Opium with the Straits Settlement and China, etc.* Vol. 6, *Final Report of the Royal Commission on Opium.* Vol. 7, *Supplement to the Report.* London: Eyre and Spottiswoode, 1894-95.

Harding, Geoffrey. *Opiate Addiction, Morality and Medicine: From Moral Illness to Pathological Disease.* London: Macmillan Press, 1988.

Hedley, John. *Tramps in Dark Mongolia.* London: T. Fisher Unwin, 1910.

Hoe, Susanna. *The Private Life of Old Hong Kong: Western Women in the British Colony, 1841-1941.* Hong Kong: Oxford University Press, 1991.

Hood, G.A. "An Introductory Study of Our Missionary 'Images,' 1847-1965." *Journal of the Presbyterian Historical Society of England* 13 (1966): 78-97.

Hosie, Alexander, *On the Trail of the Opium Poppy.* 2 vols. London: George Philip and Son, 1914.

Hyde, Francis E. *Far Eastern Trade, 1860-1914.* London: Adam and Charles Black, 1973.

International Opium Commission. *Report of the International Opium*

Commission, Shanghai, China, February 1 to February 26, 1909. 2 vols. Vol. 1, Report of the Proceedings. Vol. 2, Reports of the Delegations. Shanghai: North China Daily News and Herald, 1909.

Johnston, James, ed. Report of the Centenary Conference on the Protestant Missions of the World held in Exeter Hall (June 9th-19th), London, 1888. 2 vols. New York: F.H. Revell, 1888.

Kane, H. H. Opium-Smoking in America and China. New York: G.P. Putnam's Sons, 1882, Reprint New York: Arno Press, 1976.

Kennedy, Thomas L. "Mausers and the Opium Trade: The Hupeh Arsenal, 1895-1911." In Perspectives on a Changing China: Essays in Honor of Professor C. Martin Wilbur on the Occasion of His Retirement, edited by Joshua A. Fogel and William T. Rowe. Boulder: Westview Press, 1979.

Kitson Clark, G. Critical Historian. New York: Basic Books, 1967.

Latourette, Kenneth S. History of the Christian Missions in China. London: Society for Promoting Christian Knowledge, 1929.

Lim, Margaret J.B.C. "Britain and the Termination of the India-China Opium Trade, 1905-1913." Ph.D. diss., University of London, 1969.

Lodwick, Kathleen L. The CHINESE RECORDER Index: A Guide to Christian Missions in Asia, 1867-1941. 2 vols. Wilmington, Del.: Scholarly Resources, 1986.

MacGillivray, Donald, ed. A Century of Protestant Missions (1807-1907). Shanghai: American Presbyterian Mission Press, 1907.

Merlin, Mark David. On the Trail of the Ancient Opium Poppy. Rutherford, N.J.: Fairleigh Dickinson University Press, 1984.

Moore, W.J. The Other Side of the Opium Question. London: J. and A. Churchill, 1882.

Morse, Hosea Ballou. International Relations of the Chinese Empire. 3 vols. London: Longmans, Green, 1910-18.

——. Trade and Administration of the Chinese Empire. London: Longmans, Green, 1913.

Moule, Arthur E. New China and Old: Personal Recollections and Observations of Thirty Years. London: Seeley, 1902.

North China Herald. Jan. 1890—Dec. 1916.

"Opium Cure." Chinese Medical Missionary Journal 4 (Dec. 1890): 249-53.

Owen, David E. British Opium Policy in China and India. New Haven: Yale University Press, 1934, reprint New York: Archon Books, 1968.

Park, William H., M.D., comp. *Opinions of Over 100 Physicians on the Use of Opium in China.* Shanghai: American Presbyterian Mission Press, 1899.

Parker, Edward H. *John Chinaman and a Few Others.* London: John Murray, 1909.

Pelcovits, Nathan A. *Old China Hands and the Foreign Office.* New York: American Institute of Pacific Relations, 1948.

Pruitt, Ida. *Daughter of Han: The Autobiography of a Chinese Working Woman.* Stanford: Stanford University Press, 1945.

Rees, John David. *India: The Real India.* Boston: J.B. Millet, 1910.

Reid, Donald N. "A Behar Planter on the Opium Question." *Asiatic Review* 42: 42-43.

Remer, C.F. *Foreign Trade of China.* Shanghai: Commerical Press, 1926, reprint Taipei: Ch'eng Wen, 1967.

Robertson-Scott, J.W. *The People of China: Their Country, History, Life, Ideas and Relations with the Foreigners.* London: Methuen, 1900.

Roth, Cecil. *The Sassoon Dynasty.* London: Robert Hale, 1941.

Rowntree, Joshua. *The Imperial Drug Trade: A Re-statement of the Opium Question in the Light of Recent Evidence and New Developments in the East.* London: Methuen, 1905.

———. *The Opium Habit in the East: A Study of the Evidence Given to the Royal Commission on Opium, 1893-4.* Westminster: P.S. King and Son, 1895.

Sargent, A.J. *Anglo-Chinese Commerce and Diplomacy (Mainly in the Nineteenth Century).* Oxford: Clarendon Press, 1907.

Scott, J.M. *The White Poppy: A History of Opium.* London: Heinemann, 1969.

Shen T'ung-sheng, ed. *Kuang Hsu Cheng-yao* [Important Political Events of the Kuang-hsu Reign]. Shanghai: Ch'ung-i-t'ang, 1909.

Spence, Jonathan. "Opium Smoking in Ch'ing China," In *Conflict and Control in Late Imperial China,* ed. Frederic Wakeman Jr. and Carolyn Grant. Berkeley: University of California Press, 1975.

Sultzberger, Hartmann Henry. *All About Opium.* London: by the author, 1884.

Teng Ssu-yu and John K. Fairbank. *China's Response to the West.* New York: Antheneum, 1968.

Towns, Charles. *Habits That Handicap: The Menace of Opium, Alcohol, and Tobacco, and the Remedy.* New York: Century, 1915.

U.S. Congress. Senate. *Opium Problem.* 61st Cong., 2d sess., 1910. S. Doc. 377.

U.S. War Department. Bureau of Insular Affairs. *Report of the Committee Appointed by the Philippine Commission to Investigate the Use of Opium and the Traffic Therein and the Rules, Ordinances and Laws Regulating Such Use and Traffic in Japan, Formosa, Shanghai, Hongkong, Saigon, Singapore, Burmah, Java and the Philippine Islands.* Washington: GPO, 1905.

Walker, William O., III. *Opium and Foreign Policy: The Anglo-American Search for Order in Asia, 1912-1954.* Chapel Hill: University of North Carolina Press, 1991.

Waung, W.S.K. *The Controversy: Opium and Sino-British Relations, 1858-1887.* Typescript. Hong Kong: Lung Men Press, 1977.

Wilder, George D. "China's Attack on the Opium Problem." *Biblioteca Sacra* (Oberlin) 72 (Apr. 1915): 208-34.

Willoughby, W.W. *Opium as an International Problem: The Geneva Conferences.* Baltimore: Johns Hopkins Press, 1925.

Wright, Hamilton. "Report on the Opium Conference at Shanghai." *Proceedings of the American Society for International Law,* (1909): 89-94.

Wright, Mary C., ed. *China in Revolution: The First Phase, 1900-1913.* New Haven: Yale University Press, 1968.

Wu Wen-tsao. *The Chinese Opium Question in British Opinion and Action.* New York: Academy Press, 1928.

Yu En-te. *Chung-kuo chin yen fa-ling pien-ch'ien shih* [History of the Changes in Chinese Anti-Opium Laws]. Shanghai: China Press, 1934.

Zabriskie, Alexander C. *Bishop Brent: Crusader for Christian Unity.* Philadelphia: Westminster Press, 1948.

Index

addiction, 40-42, 65; cures and attempted cures for, 18, 29, 35, 37-38, 43, 46-48, 66, 78, 112, 119-21, 130-36, 139-40, 152, 154, 164; reasons for 20, 93-94

addicts: Chinese, 4, 117-21; amount smoked, 17-18, 189 n 19; artisans, 42; as converts/ church members, 2-3, 33, 47, 54, 66, 69, 128, 181; beggars, 24; children, 9, 18, 21, 36, 41-42, 47-48, 65, 110; coolies, 21, 42, 92, 134, 159; gentry, 22; government officials, 21-22, 42, 120; lifespan, 21; merchants, 42; moral sense of, 40, 92; peasants, 22-24, 42; physical condition, 20-21, 24-26, 40, 41, 92, 190 n 31; reasons for use, 19-21; social status, 21, 40, 92; statistics, 17-19, 36, 139; urban, 42; women, 18, 22-24, 36, 41, 47-48, 139; in India, 4, 73-74; among Westerners, 4, 93-94, 99

Albert, Dr. José, 109

Alcock, Sir Rutherford, 60, 61, 190 n 13

Alexander, Joseph G., 58-62, 77, 81, 89, 141

All About Opium, 83

Allen, Clement F.R., 91, 106

America. *See* United States/ Americans

American Baptist Missionary Union, 36, 106, 135

American Board of Commissioners for Foreign Missions, 36, 131

American Civil War, 4

American Methodist Mission, 32

American Presbyterian Mission, 36, 39, 47, 48

American Protestant Episcopal Missionary Society, 52

American Southern Methodist Mission, 39, 49

American Southern Presbyterian Mission, 41

Amoy, 14, 15, 17, 60, 168

Anderson, Dr. Peter, 41

Andrew, George, 155

Anglo-Oriental Society for the Suppression of the Opium Trade. *See* Society for the Suppression of the Opium Trade

Anhwei, 14, 68, 137, 163, 164, 169, 178

Anking, Anhwei, 168-70, 178

anti-opium activists: British, 8,

www.ingramcontent.com/pod-product-compliance
Lightning Source LLC
Chambersburg PA
CBHW020609270326
41927CB00005B/241